Is There a Teacher
in the House?

Is There a Teacher in the House?

You and Your Child's Faith

by
William H. Bray

Beacon Hill Press of Kansas City
Kansas City, Missouri

Copyright 1987
by Beacon Hill Press of Kansas City

ISBN: 083-411-2183

Printed in the
United States of America

Cover: Ratcliff/Vail

10 9 8 7 6 5 4 3 2 1

To

my beloved wife and partner
in Christian parenting,
Judy,

and the two precious "talents"
God has entrusted into our care,
Krista and Brandon

Contents

Foreword

One fellow vowed to be versatile or nothing, and to his disappointment, he ended up both! Not so for the leader of England's 18th-century revival.

I visited the City Road residence where John Wesley lived the last decade of his life. After climbing the narrow staircase, I entered his study, where evidence of his versatility abounds.

There is a self-designed wooden saddle, equipped with a small ledge to balance the books he read as he traveled by horseback to preaching assignments. In addition there is an ingenious "shock therapy" apparatus, which, I was told, he recommended for most ailments. Then there are the many books he authored on a wide range of subjects—from politics to medical remedies.

I departed, wondering how one man could have become so creative in so many different areas. So intrigued was I that upon my return I read nearly a dozen books on the life and teachings of this "Renaissance man." That was a rich and inspirational experience.

But never did I consider Wesley to be an expert on child raising—nor did the sources I consulted. After all, he wasn't a parent.

It was then that I was exposed to William Bray's book manuscript. This author has effectively elaborated on yet another aspect of the reformer's versatility.

I was pleasantly surprised by what I read, and you will be, too. Truly, the "man of Aldersgate" has offered timeless and timely admonitions to parents, admonitions like:

"Instruct your children, early, plainly, frequently, and patiently."

"Never . . . give a child any thing that it cries for. [Otherwise] you pay him for crying."

These Wesleyan principles are laid before readers in a well-organized, succinct manner and placed on a backdrop of Scripture. In addition the author interlaces ideas of contemporary scholars. I was specifically impressed with Haim Ginott's distinction between "green," "yellow," and "red" behavior, along with how parents should respond to each.

William Bray also offers meaningful illustrations that are drawn from his own family setting. I smiled at four-year-old-daughter Krista's response to her father's question: "[Does] anybody else live in heaven with God and Jesus?" Her answer: "No. *[Pause.]* Maybe little children."

Undeniably, parenting is a vital subject. Wesley claimed that it has a direct bearing on the survival of the Church of Jesus Christ.

Biblical insights that assist us in this important task are welcome. William Bray commendably shares such insights.

—Jon Johnston, Ph.D.
Pepperdine University

Preface

Psychologist James Dobson describes the passing of Christian faith from one generation to the next in terms of a three-man relay race. Our earthly father runs his prescribed lap around the track of life, carrying the baton, which is the gospel of Jesus Christ. He gets it into our hands, and then we run our lap around the track. Now it becomes our responsibility, as parents, to get the baton—the gospel—into the hands of our children. Nothing else, says Dobson, even comes close to the importance of that responsibility. If our children don't get the baton and carry it with them, then nothing else in life really matters.[1]

Obviously we don't give our children Christian faith. The Bible says it is a gift of God (Eph. 2:8). But we do inspire the faith of our children. We can influence whether those sons or daughters of ours will receive and exercise Christian faith for themselves. This book is written for Christian parents who desire to maximize this influence on their children. You might say it is for parents who wish to improve their "handoff" of the baton.

The child-rearing method being proposed here is drawn from one of church history's most famous figures: John Wesley, father of Methodism. Surprisingly, this childless churchman of 18th-century England had a lot to say about child rearing. Even more surprisingly, many of the principles Wesley believed and taught are still principles that can help us today as Christian parents.

This book is written from a pastor's perspective—a pastor (you guessed it) in the Wesleyan theological tradition. Years in the pastorate taught me to be concerned about and responsible for not only my own two children but also the children of my parishioners. As a pastor, I witnessed the anxiety, regret, guilt, and even desperation Christian parents sometimes feel regarding their children. I have come to the conclusion that parents need to be better informed, both theologically and developmentally, about Christian nurture in the family setting. Hopefully these pages will supply some of that information. My prayer is that God will help us keep our families at the very top of our list of priorities. If we don't, then Dobson is right: "Nothing else in life really matters."

1

Passing the Faith Along

Have you heard the one about the psychologist who wrote his thesis on how to bring up children? At the time, he was not married and his lecture read, "Twelve Requirements for How to Bring Up Children." He later married, had his first child, and his lecture title was changed to read, "Twelve Suggestions for How to Bring Up Children." After he and his wife had their second child, his lecture title was changed again to read, "Twelve Hints on How to Bring Up Children." When the third child arrived, he stopped giving lectures on that subject altogether!

Children have a way of doing away with our nice, neat theories about child rearing, don't they? It reminds me of Sisyphus, in Greek mythology, whose eternal fate was to push a large boulder up a hill. Every time he would get it to the top and was about ready to push it over, the boulder would shift sideways and go rolling back down the hill. Similarly, just about the time we think we have child rearing all figured out, something happens, and we watch those wonderful theories of ours go rolling back down the hill. Perhaps you can identify with the "Sisyphus syndrome."

Raising children is undoubtedly one of the most difficult jobs in the world. It has been said that parents teach in the toughest school in the world—The School for Making People. Parents are the board of education, principal, classroom teacher, and janitor all rolled into two—or even just one, in the case of single parents. Your school has no holidays, vacations, unions, promotions, or pay raises. You are on duty or at least on call 24 hours a day, 365 days a year, for at least 18 years per child. In addition, most of you have to work with an administration that has two bosses.[1] It's enough to make a parent go on strike and circle the house with a picket sign, isn't it? This is not to say that parenting is not rewarding and meaningful—but pure pleasure? Forget it!

The difficulty of raising children is complicated by the fact that not one of them comes with a set of instructions. Have you noticed that? I witnessed the births of both our children, and neither time did the doctors hand over a set of instructions. Think about that for a moment! What more difficult and demanding job is there than taking full responsibility for a little person who is almost totally helpless—with no instructions? It's kind of like—if you're a human being, you ought to know how to raise one. Unfortunately, that is not the case. Becoming a parent does not automatically confer upon any of us the know-how and skills to raise healthy, responsible children. This is why many psychologists and family therapists today feel that parents need to be trained for their job.[2] Included in this group needing training are Christian parents, since they have the added responsibility of Christian nurture and instruction (Eph. 6:4).

The Family Blueprint: Your Design for Disciple Making

Family therapist Virginia Satir states that parents face two big questions: "*What* kind of a human being do I want my child to become?" and "*How* am I going to use myself and my spouse to make that happen?" The answers become the basis for what she calls "The Family Blueprint: Your Design for Peoplemaking." We've changed that just slightly to read, "The Family Blueprint: Your Design for Disciple Making."

14

Satir declares that every parent has answers to these questions, whether stated or not, clear or vague.[3]

Why not take a sheet of paper right now and jot down your answers to her two questions? You may want to write out your answers in paragraph form or number items separately. The first time I did this, my wife and I had taken a few days vacation, without the kids, to go skiing. Back in the lodge one evening, I took a pencil and some paper and drew something like this:

The Family Blueprint: My Design for Disciple Making

What Do I Want My Child to Become?	How Can I Seek to Make That Happen?

Two things soon were discovered. One, such an exercise produces motivation for providing good spiritual training in the home. When you see *what* you would like your child to become, you can more easily plan *how* to structure faith activities in the home.[4] The second thing is that such an exercise is not easy. Oh, I answered the first question easily enough, but that's because most parents have some idea of the kind of person they want their child to become. For example:

What Do I Want My Child to Become?	How Can I Seek to Make That Happen?
1. I want my child to become a Christian and then to be committed to the church through faithful attendance, involvement, and service.	
2. I want my child to be a caring individual, a person who will be sensitive to the needs of others and willing to help.	
3. I want my child to be a kind, courteous, and responsible human being.	
4. Etcetera.	

The real difficulty began with the second heading: *"How Can I Seek to Make That Happen?"* I had never really thought about it that way before, but the question gripped me that night and has done so ever since. That evening in the ski lodge, I determined more than ever to give more attention to the *How?* of Christian parenting. This book is partly the result of that decision.

A Church Within a House

Several years ago in our first pastorate, I responded to a garage sale advertisement in the newspaper. It seemed that an elderly lady was selling the library of her deceased minister-husband. Among the several books I purchased were three books of sermons by the renowned 20th-century preacher, Harry Emerson Fosdick. One of his sermons was titled "Family Religion" and was based on "the church that is in their house" (Rom. 16:5; 1 Cor. 16:19; cf. Col. 4:15; Philemon 2). In the sermon, Fosdick said that religion organizes itself in different ways. For example, there is "personal religion," which we carry around inside of us. There is "ecclesiastical religion," institutionalized in our churches. Then there is "family religion which, when it is at its best, floods a home with light and makes the relationships therein sacred and beautiful. It creates a church within a house."[5]

That concept caused some thought. "Family religion . . . creates a church within a house." We don't hear and talk as much about family religion as we do the other two types. We hear and talk a lot about personal religion and church religion, but not about family religion. Even many people who are not particularly concerned about themselves spiritually understand and demonstrate the need for "ecclesiastical religion." Many of them send their children to church every Sunday, for example. They firmly believe that the church has something their sons and daughters desperately need, though they're not always sure what that is.

May we talk candidly? Parents who send their children to church but do not go themselves simply do not realize what they are doing. One father sent his little preschool-age daughter to our church with the message that if her Sunday School class ever needed anything, to let him know. The urge came (though not carried out) to respond: "She doesn't need anything but you to bring her to church, not send her!" The reasoning behind that father's actions—and the many like him—is clear: Religion is the responsibility of the church. How terrible! Doesn't that father know that the family is the most basic unit of society? Doesn't that man realize that his daughter is in continuous contact with the family, not the church? In fact, it's been said that the average church has a

17

child 1 percent of the time, the family 83 percent of the time, and the school the remainder.[6] Even if these figures are only vaguely true, the fact is that the home has a child for far more time than any other institution.

Let it be known loudly and clearly that the following are firm beliefs:

- Christian parents are called to bring up their children in the Christian faith.

- Christian education begins in the home, not the church.

- While the church has an obligation to nurture children in the Christian faith, parents do not have the right to abdicate their responsibility and expect the church to nurture their children for them.

- Church training, at best, is only an extension or supplement to the training that children receive at home from their parents.

- No matter where you look in our Judeo-Christian heritage, it is parents who have the primary responsibility for bringing up their children in the faith.[7]

Let's talk a little bit about that last one. In the Old Testament, the home was the center of religious education, and parents were the teachers. Take a look at Exod. 12:26-27; Deut. 4:9-10; 6:7, 20-25; 11:19; 32:7, 46; Ps. 78:3-6; and Prov. 22:6 for starters. You might be surprised. In the New Testament, Christian nurture was the fundamental duty of parents. In fact, there is no mention of religious education and schools for children in the New Testament. The assumption is that the only training that really matters is given within the home.[8] Take special note of Eph. 6:4. In the 4th century, Early Church Father John Chrysostom wrote a treatise titled *On the*

Right Way for Parents to Bring Up Their Children. From the 1st to the 15th centuries, ecclesiastical pronouncements condemned parents for neglecting their children's nurture. Parents were strongly urged to assume their God-given responsibility.

In the 16th century, Martin Luther emphasized parental instruction, urging fathers to instruct their children in religion at least once a week. For Luther, the first duty of parenthood was religious education. John Calvin preached often on the responsibility parents had for the religious education of their children. In the 17th century the Puritans, on both sides of the Atlantic, took seriously the responsibility of parents for the Christian nurture of children. In 1642 Massachusetts even passed a law requiring parents to instruct their children in the principles of religion at least once a week. In the 19th century the father of the Christian education movement in the United States, Horace Bushnell, declared, "Let every Christian father and mother understand that when their child is three years old that they have done more than half of all they will ever do for their character."[9]

And so on down through church history. Clearly, the importance of the family for the development of religious faith is well established in both Scripture and tradition. Even though the idea and practice of family religion is certainly nothing new, it seems self-evident that family life today demands a new emphasis on it. We need a return to the biblical and traditional understanding of "the church that is in [our] house."

"The Grand Desideratum"

There is one other name to be added alongside the names of Chrysostom, Luther, Calvin, and Bushnell. In fact, this person will guide our discussion throughout the book. This man lived in 18th-century England. He had a lot to say about family religion; yet surprisingly, he had no children of his own. His name was John Wesley, the father of Methodism. Wesley called family religion "the grand desideratum among the Methodists."[10] Now you're probably wondering what in the world "desideratum" means—a "grand desideratum" at that. Mr. Webster defines the word "desideratum" to mean "something desired as essential."[11] In other words, John Wesley regarded family religion as absolutely essential! He did not consider it optional, as we would consider electric windows, power locks, and a tilt steering wheel on a new car. He considered it standard equipment in the Christian life.

Not only did Wesley believe family religion to be essential, he believed it to be "shamefully wanting" among the early Methodists.[12] He also believed that this neglect would seriously and adversely affect the church. "What will the consequence be," he asked, "if family religion be neglected? —if care be not taken of the rising generation? Will not the present revival of religion in a short time die away?"[13] So important was this to him that he instructed his Methodist preachers to promote it in the homes of their parishioners. One of the stated questions Wesley asked preachers seeking admission to the Methodist Conference was, "Will you diligently and earnestly instruct the children, and visit from house to house?"[14] If anyone objected as to their gift for doing such a thing, Wesley responded, "Gift or no gift, you are to do it; else you are not called to be a Methodist Preacher."[15] In the Methodist Conference of 1768, Wesley challenged his preachers with the necessity of family religion: "But what shall we do for the rising generation? Unless we take care of this, the present revival will . . . last only the age of a man."[16]

Now you're probably thinking: Why would anyone today be interested in the child-rearing views of an 18th-century churchman who had no children of his own and whose marriage was—well—not so great? By the way, Wesley gave out a lot of advice on marriage, too. Someone has called the idea of John Wesley giving advice on marriage "grimly humorous."[17] If that is true for his advice on marriage, what do we call his advice on child rearing? The credibility of a childless man on the subject of child rearing is certainly questionable, isn't it? Wesley knew that, too. On one occasion he spoke to a crowd of people about family religion, and, in his words, "Some still made that very silly answer, 'Oh he has no children of his own!'" Sounds like Wesley had been stung by that criticism more than once. Listen to his reply. "Neither had St. Paul, nor (that we know) any of the apostles. What then? Were they therefore unable to instruct parents? No so. They were able to instruct everyone that had a soul to be saved."[18] The man has a point, but there are three additional reasons why John Wesley has earned the right to talk to us today about family religion.

First, he was particularly interested in and committed to the religious education of the young. In addition to his Methodist preachers, societies, classes, bands, and schools, he strongly urged parents to implement religious education in the home, and provided them the resources to do so.

Second, and more specifically, Wesley earned the right to be heard because of the remarkable homelife he had in his own childhood.[19] Wesley's mature reflection on those childhood experiences helped to form child-rearing views essentially the same as those of his extraordinary mother, Susanna. Susanna Wesley ranks as one of the great matriarchs of church history. We'll talk more about her later and just briefly mention here her success in raising a large family (10 of her 19 children survived infancy). The Wesley family developed into one of the most eminent families in English history. Although her daughters were limited by the day in which they lived, they were spirited and well educated. As for her three distinguished sons—Samuel, John, and Charles—the eminence they attained in several fields speaks volumes about their homelife.[20]

There is a third reason why John Wesley should be heard. Even though he considered family religion to be lacking among early Methodists, the truth is that the early Methodist people were distinguished for their "sense of family." One of the reasons early Methodism grew so rapidly is that Christian faith was communicated from father to son, brother to sister, and so on to the most distant kinsfolk. There was a "homeliness" about early Methodism, which may have been due to its emphasis on intimate sharing of thought and feeling.[21]

Please do not misunderstand. When we say that John Wesley can tell us something about Christian child rearing today, there is much more he cannot tell us. After all, two centuries separate him from us. The 18th century had a very limited understanding of childhood, and Wesley was no exception. On the other hand, many of the principles he believed and taught are principles that can still help us as Christian parents today. This is what is important here. We still need someone, like John Wesley, to remind us that family religion is indeed "the grand desideratum"!

Theology AND Psychology

As Christian parents, we obviously look to the Bible to help us understand Christian faith. This does not mean that we cannot learn about faith from other sources as well. While the Bible teaches us "what" we are to believe, psychology helps us understand "how" we come to believe. Psychology helps parents understand child development. This does not mean that theology and psychology are equal in their capacity to inform Christian faith. Far from it! Someone has written, "Man, according to the Bible, is to be understood from above downward, not from below upward. . . . Only when

Man has been understood theologically . . . can we understand him psychologically."[22] Amen to that! After a solid theological foundation has been laid, parents can then look to psychology for considerable help in understanding the ways their children believe.

Effective Christian parenting requires both theological *and* psychological understanding! We parents must know what the Bible says about Christian faith, but we also need to know how our children exercise faith at different periods in their lives. In the next chapter, we're going to talk a little bit about this. Let's leave Wesley for a while and pick him up again in chapter 3. Before we do, let's remind ourselves one more time: *Family religion is "the grand desideratum"!*

DISCUSSION QUESTIONS

1. Write out and/or discuss your answers to "The Family Blueprint: My Design for Disciple Making."
2. Discuss the idea that parents need to be trained for their job.
3. What is the relationship of home and church in family nurture?
4. What does the idea of "family religion" mean to you?
5. Discuss the significance of Wesley's statement: "Family religion is the grand desideratum."
6. Discuss the statement: "Effective Christian parenting requires both theological *and* psychological understanding!"

2

Faith Never Changes— or Does It?

How did you come to know what you now believe? Obviously your faith has not always been the same as it is right now. This is because our capacity to understand will change as we grow. Try a little exercise. Consider the doctrine of heaven. Try to recall the earliest picture you had of heaven. Then trace the development of your thinking about heaven since that time. Take a sheet of paper and answer the following questions. Your paper might look like this:

Heaven
---

1. What did I believe in the past?

2. What do I presently think?

3. What caused any changes in my thinking?

When you finish, try doing the same with other doctrines, beliefs, or experiences. What did you believe in the past? What do you presently think? What caused any changes in your thinking? A group of parents in one of our churches did this. When it came time to share their answers, most of them were amazed at what they once believed about heaven (as children) and what they now believe about heaven (as adults). Their earliest pictures of heaven included everything from harp playing to cloud sitting, but not one of them believe that about heaven now! This little exercise is designed to show us how faith changes as we grow.

The notion of "development" has come quite late in the history of ideas. Though people have always been aware that persons change as they move from childhood through adolescence into adulthood, it has only been in this century that stages of the life cycle have been elaborately studied and defined. We now have extensive information about all kinds of development: physical, intellectual, educational, social, and moral development, to name just a few.

It comes as no surprise that the church has been profoundly influenced by ideas of human development. For example, consider the graded materials used in our Sunday Schools. We know enough not to pass out adult quarterlies in the primary class. We understand that children are not ready for such materials. This is because a person's readiness for learning will gradually unfold in stages of increased intellectual capacities and widening social experiences.[1] We've heard about this, but how well do we really know it?

Think, for a moment, how utterly foreign many expressions of biblical faith are to modern men and women, young people, and children. Some years ago a group of communication students from one Christian college surveyed passersby at a local shopping center. When the people were asked the question, "What do you think of first when you hear the word 'saved'?" the most popular reply was, "It's what I wish I'd done with my last paycheck." When asked about the word "redemption," most of them mentioned the then-popular Green Stamps[2] that could be redeemed for gas, gifts, or merchandise. This communication problem is partly due to the cultural gap separating our day and Bible days. In order to bridge this cultural gap, an attempt must be made to translate some of the more difficult expressions of biblical faith into modern language. This is precisely the reason for newer translations of the Bible. The point is this: If we adults sometimes have problems understanding the Bible, what about our children? The problem becomes magnified where children are concerned. With them, there is not only a cultural gap, usually greater than for many of us, but also one involving their developmental stage as well.[3] Even a familiar expression of biblical faith for us is often a problem for them because of their limited understanding and experience.

Effective parenting—and that includes Christian parents—requires some knowledge of child development. Once we understand what our children are capable of and not capable of, we can provide them with better Christian nurture. There is nothing more important than to see our children grow up to receive Jesus Christ as Lord and Savior for themselves. Everything else in life pales in significance. We need to do everything we can to make sure that happens. This is why I want to introduce you to a couple of men who have helped me understand our children better. The first is James Fowler, and the second is John Westerhoff.

The Faith Development Theory of James W. Fowler

Dr. James W. Fowler is director of the Center for Faith Development at Emory University. He has developed a theory that shows how people exercise faith at different periods or stages throughout life. His theory has helped me immensely as a Christian parent.

Faith development or growth in faith can be compared to the rings on a tree. Have you ever seen a tree cut down and then counted the rings to see how old it is? A tree acquires one ring at a time in a slow and gradual manner. A tree does not skip rings. As a tree grows, it does not eliminate rings but adds each new ring to the ones before, always maintaining the previous rings as it grows. A tree grows if the proper environment is provided; if such an environment is lacking, the tree's growth is stunted until the proper environment exists. Finally, a tree with one ring is just as much a tree as a tree with four rings. The same processes apply to faith.[4]

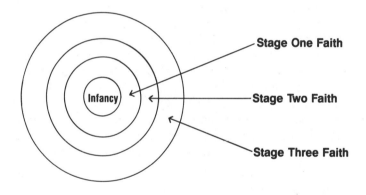

Faith development or growth in faith does *not* mean that we grow into Christian faith! Eph. 2:8 says clearly that Christian faith is a gift of God. What it does mean is that God has created each of us with perceptions or understandings that unfold gradually and in orderly fashion throughout life, in matters of faith and morality.[5] Let's talk about these stages of faith, birth through adolescence, in relation to our children.

Infancy

The journey of faith, Fowler asserts, begins in infancy. The tendency is to think just the opposite, that faith begins when children are old enough to go to school—first grade. Not so. His thesis is that the pilgrimage of faith begins the moment a child arrives in this world, for faith begins as "trust." A sense of trust is communicated to the infant through the quality and consistency of care provided by parents or parent-like adults. The child senses whether this strange new world is safe and dependable. This learning of trust underlies all that comes later in faith development.[6]

If a parent's attentiveness to the infant's needs is helping shape the faith of that child, then so is a parent's inattentiveness. The infant does not learn to trust when needs are consistently delayed or when the quality of care is consistently poor. If parents are grudging, hostile, impatient, or anxious, then their handling of the infant may also be rough, jerky, abrupt, and fumbling. This tends to confuse and frighten the child. What the infant needs is handling that expresses love and confidence.[7] Obviously, we're not talking about the initial clumsiness of new parents, but the prolonged effects of poor care. This is when the infant learns mistrust, which tends to undermine faith development.

Stage One Faith (2 or 3 years old to 6 or 7 years old)

Stage one faith typically includes children, ages two or three to six or seven years. Intellectually, it is a prereasoning period. Knowing is primarily by intuition. The stage one child typically sees just one aspect of a situation at a time, which usually leads to incomplete or wrong judgments.[8] For example, if you place two equal-length pencils side by side, and push one slightly in front of the other, the stage one child will usually say that the one is longer than the other.[9] This child can see that two clay balls have the same amount of clay, and yet after he watches the one ball be flattened, the child will usually say that the unsmashed ball now has more clay—another example of stage one thinking.[10]

Perhaps the most important characteristic of stage one thinking is something called irreversible thought. It is difficult for the child to undo something mentally. For example, if we as adults were to receive directions for driving to a friend's house across town, we would simply follow the directions to get there with no problems. When ready to return home, we would take advantage of "reversible" thought and retrace our route. A stage one child has difficulty doing this because his thought is irreversible.

Their underdeveloped understanding causes stage one children to see things in short episodes. For example, they will remember episodes from a television show, but not the narrative line of the story. Their ability to take someone else's point of view is also very limited. For a parent to say, "Just think how that makes Mommy feel," is to ask them to do what they really cannot do. If they see tears, for example, they will respond with sympathy to the mood, but it is still a very elementary sympathy. I vividly remember my two children, at this stage, coming up and consoling me after my mother's death. They would put their arms around me and ask, "What's the matter, Daddy?" Then they would hug and kiss me. They really didn't know how I felt, but they could see that I was crying, and they responded to the tears. Thinking at stage one is basically self-centered.

The really important people in the life of a stage one child are parents and family. Acquaintances and relations outside the family circle do impact the child, but not to the extent that the family does.[11] At stage one, there is a strong relationship between a child's idea of God and his relationship with parents. Psychologist James Dobson tells about his son, Ryan, during these years. Ryan was called upon to say the blessing before one of their meals. He sputtered out,

"I love you, Daddy. Amen."[12] Isn't it a sobering thought, parent, to think that our stage one children associate us with God?

Stage one also represents a premoral stage of development. The rightness and wrongness or goodness and badness of actions are understood in terms of punishment and reward. Good is what brings pleasure. Bad is what brings pain. Since stage one children have difficulty taking someone else's point of view, they really do not understand motives. For example, they see the child who breaks five glasses accidentally as deserving more punishment than the child who breaks one glass on purpose. The consequences of an act are all-important.

Finally, stage one children have trouble separating fact from fantasy, the real from the unreal. Consequently, they have trouble distinguishing between symbols and reality. Have you ever stopped to consider how much the Christian life involves symbols, rituals, metaphors, and the like? For example, baptism symbolizes the gift of new life in Christ. Communion symbolizes the death, presence, and coming again of our Lord. Stage one children have difficulty looking past these symbols to what they represent. The symbolic and the real are linked. Symbols take on a magical quality for them.[13]

One morning at the breakfast table I told Krista (almost four at the time) a story Fowler uses in his interviews with stage one children. It's a story about a brother and sister who wander away at a family picnic and get lost. I asked Krista how she would help her brother, Brandon (almost two), not be afraid. Notice some of the characteristics we have been describing in her responses:

Krista (at first changed the subject, but then said): I'd say, "We'll be back home in a minute."

Me: Anything else?

Krista: I'd say, "Daddy will be here in just a minute."

Me: Would you give him anything?

Krista: I'd give him some food from the trees—but I couldn't reach it.

Me: Anything else?

Krista: No.

Me (changing the subject): What do you think God might look like?

Krista: Like Jesus.

Me: What does Jesus look like?

Krista: I don't know. I don't know.

Me: Have you ever seen a picture of Jesus?

Krista: No.

Me: Where does Jesus live?

Krista: In heaven.

Me: And where is heaven at?

Krista: Up, way above the clouds in the sky.

Me: Who lives in heaven?

Krista: God and Jesus.

Me: Anybody else live in heaven with God and Jesus?

Krista: No. *[Pause.]* Maybe little children.

Me: How do you get up to heaven?

Krista: Jesus reaches down with His big hand and picks them up. *[Note: Krista had a Bible story book at the time with a picture of God's big hand.]*

Me: How do mommies and daddies get up to heaven?

Krista: Jesus has a bigger hand to pick them up!

I cannot emphasize enough the importance of Christian parenting at this stage. It is a critical time, to say the least.

One reason is that parents are the most important people in the child's life. This begins to change at stage two, as we shall see.

Stage Two Faith (6 or 7 years old to 11 or 12 years old)

Stage two faith is typical of elementary-age children, 6 or 7 to 11 or 12 years. Intellectually, reasoning and thought (beyond intuition) are now possible, but thinking still depends on what they can see, touch, taste, smell, or hear. Whereas stage one children tend to see just one aspect of a situation at a time, stage two children can consider more than one aspect. For example, stage two children know that one of two equal-length pencils pushed slightly ahead of the other does not make it longer. If they watch you flatten one of two equal-amount clay balls, they understand that both balls still have the same amount of clay. Stage two children are also able to mentally undo something that has been done; for example, they can retrace their route back home from a friend's house.

One of the major characteristics of stage two children is the hearing, telling, and retelling of stories—stories about school, playmates, adventures, you name it. This does not mean that stage one children do not like to hear or tell stories, but they usually do not achieve the relative mastery of storytelling that stage two children do. Generally, however, even those stage two stories are quite flat and are meant to be taken literally; they sometimes tax the patience of even the most attentive adults. Stories for stage two children are their way of making sense out of their world and giving meaning to their experiences.[14]

This hearing and telling of stories has important implications for Christian parenting. Since it is human nature to order our lives in accordance with a story, parents need to tell, retell, and even role-play Bible stories with their children.[15]

Fowler illustrates this principle through an interview he had with a man in his 30s who recalled, as a young boy, how his mother would always read a Bible story to him before his afternoon nap. One of his favorite stories was Samuel's call in the house of God (1 Samuel 1—3). The man admitted he felt a closeness to the boy, Samuel, as Samuel served in the house of the Lord. As the Scripture story goes, Samuel on three different occasions heard a call in the night. He went each time to Eli, the high priest, thinking that Eli had called him. After the third time, Eli perceived that God was addressing the boy, so he instructed Samuel to answer the next time, "Speak, Lord, for thy servant hears" (3:9, RSV). The man in Fowler's interview recalled that as an older child and adolescent, he frequently woke up in the middle of the night to find himself praying, "Speak, Lord, for thy servant hears." Not surprisingly, Fowler says, this man is a minister and theologian today.

At stage two, the ability to consider someone else's point of view is beginning to replace the self-centeredness of stage one. The influence of the family, so strong at stage one, is now joined by relationships with teachers and other school authorities, friends, and their friends' families. Stage two children strongly identify with others who are like themselves socially, ethnically, racially, and religiously.[16] An illustration of this is an incident from a certain well-to-do family in another country. At bedtime, the eight-year-old boy said his prayers with his mother but refused to pray for "Johnny the Tinker." In that country a tinker was something like a social outcast.[17] The boy just could not identify with someone of another social class.

Although some personal judgments are forming at stage two, children still look to trusted adults like parents and teachers, as well as to older brothers and sisters, for authority. Morally, a strong sense of fairness is beginning to emerge. This is largely due to their ability to consider someone else's point of view. If you're serving chocolate cake to stage two children, you'd better not give more to one than to the other, or you're liable to hear about it. Many a mom has heard the words, "Hey, that's not fair! He's got more than me!" The child's sense of fairness has been violated.

Finally, stage two children generally understand that symbols and metaphors refer to something else, but they tend to understand them literally. For example, when the Bible talks about "the hand of God" or "the eyes of the Lord," adults understand that this does not mean that God has literal hands or eyes. Stage two children tend to interpret such statements literally. They picture God as having humanlike features and qualities. When asked, "What does God look like?" one 10-year-old girl answered like this:

> Well, I don't know. But do you want me to tell you what I imagine that he looks like? I imagine that he's an old man with a white beard and white hair wearing a long robe and that the clouds are his floor and he has a throne. And he has all these people and there's angels around him. And there's all the good people, angels and —and um, cupids and that he has like—I guess I—he has a nice face, nice blue eyes. He can't be all white, you know, he has to—he has blue eyes and he's forgiving. And I guess that's the way I think he is.[18]

Stage Three Faith (11 or 12 years old to late adolescence)

Stage three faith basically covers the period of adolescence. Intellectually, stage three adolescents are beginning to think in terms of concepts and ideas. They do not have to experience something, as do stage two children, in order to reason about it. Fowler uses the analogy of a stream. Stage two children speak from within the flow of experience but do not step outside the stream for reflection. Stage three adolescents usually have the ability to mentally step outside the flow of life's stream and reflect on the patterns and meanings that they see in the stream.

34

Stage three is an identity-seeking stage. Not only are adolescents able to consider someone else's point of view, but also they are very concerned about what others think of them. They tend to feel that everyone else is looking at them. Everyone, and especially peers, becomes a mirror in which they see themselves. Needless to say, it is a terribly self-conscious time.

The influences on adolescents are many: family, peers, media, school, work, church, and perhaps many other "theys." Adolescents' moral judgments are sometimes based on fulfilling the expectations of these people. The motive is to please those who matter greatly to them and not to disappoint others' opinions and expectations.

Because stage three adolescents are greatly influenced by what others think, it tends to be a conformist stage. They often *feel* deeply about their beliefs and values but typically have difficulty *putting into words* why they believe what they believe. This is because adolescent faith is very dependent on the faith of other important people in their lives—people like parents, peers, pastor, Sunday School teacher, and so on. Toward late adolescence and early adulthood, faith tends to become less dependent on other people and much more personal. The older teens or young adults usually have less difficulty stating why they believe what they believe.

Not only are adolescents concerned about what their friends and family think of them, but they are very concerned about what God thinks of them. They are attracted to a God who is deeply affirming and accepting of them. Whereas stage two children tend to picture God with human-like features and qualities, stage three adolescents tend to see God as a friend, companion, counselor, or guide. Love, caring, support, and acceptance are important qualities in the adolescent's understanding of God. This means that at a time when others are terribly important to the formation of identity, God is potentially the most important "other" in the formation of that identity. Adolescents see themselves as they think God sees them!

Finally, symbols and metaphors are no longer taken literally, as at stage two. Adolescents understand, however naively, that symbols represent something else. They also consider symbols to be very sacred.[19]

John Westerhoff's Four Styles of Faith

Dr. John H. Westerhoff is professor of religion and education at Duke University Divinity School. He has developed a simplified version of faith development, similar to Fowler's. According to Westerhoff's theory, children move through four styles or levels of faith: experienced faith, dependent faith, searching faith, and owned faith.

Experienced Faith
(preschool through early elementary years)

To learn of the Lord as a shepherd and the biblical concept of shepherding, young children must first experience what real, live sheep are all about.[20] This is an example of "experienced" faith. This first style of faith says that the most important and fundamental form of learning is experience.

I vividly remember taking Krista and Brandon, five and three at the time, to visit a nearby sheep barn in our town. It was owned and operated by the local university. The kids looked, listened, touched, and, of course, smelled the sheep. What a time we had! Brandon even cried because he couldn't take one home. That night I purposefully read one of their Bible stories having to do with Jesus' statement, "I am the good shepherd" (John 10:11, 14). I could hardly finish for them interrupting and comparing their afternoon trip with the story.

Experienced faith is not difficult to understand when you stop to consider how much children explore, imagine, create, observe, and imitate. We get so caught up in the habit of telling things to people—especially children—that we forget the tremendous value of firsthand experience. As we grow older, we can understand things without having to experience them first—but this is not the case with children. Their thinking depends on interacting with people and things, not symbols and ideas. A child first learns Christ not as a theological statement but as a felt experience.

Dependent Faith
(elementary age through early to mid adolescence)

This style of faith is most typical of elementary-age children through early to middle adolescence. As with Fowler's theory, "dependent" (or affiliative) faith refers to the fact that faith tends to be grounded in the authority of others, like Dad, Mom, the pastor, or the Sunday School teacher. Here faith is accepted and practiced without question, which makes it a prime teaching period. At this level of faith, there is a strong need to belong and participate in the activities of the church.

Searching Faith
(mid to late adolescence through early adulthood)

Westerhoff says that there comes a time, usually in mid to late adolescence, when teenagers feel the need to understand faith for themselves. Religion of the head becomes equally important with religion of the heart. Older adolescents typically begin to think theologically and morally about life. They begin to think seriously about the Bible and ask questions about its meaning. Westerhoff calls this the period of "searching" faith. In searching faith, adolescents are struggling to understand and appreciate their faith. It cannot be Dad's or Mom's or Pastor's faith any longer, as with dependent faith. It has to become their very own. Searching faith is often triggered when teenagers leave home, go away to college, or enter the job market.

Searching faith can be a terribly insecure time for parents, but the alternative is equally disturbing: If young people remain in the dependent level of faith, they cannot make faith their very own. Consequently, there is little understanding and appreciation of faith for those adolescents. Dependent faith cannot easily withstand the challenge of secular authorities and humanistic university professors, for they can argue for their beliefs and values as convincingly as Dad, Mom, and the church can argue for theirs. If there is any consolation for parents during this time, it is to know that beyond it lies the realm of owned faith.[21]

Owned Faith
(young adulthood onward)

Theologian and philosopher Elton Trueblood has written, "A faith that has never been tested is not only not appreciated, it is not even understood."[22] Peter told some Early Church Christians, "That the trial of your faith, being much more precious than of gold that perisheth, though it be tried with fire, might be found unto praise and honour and glory at the appearing of Jesus Christ" (1 Pet. 1:7). "Owned" faith means a faith that is both understood and appreciated. I don't know of a Christian parent anywhere who does not want that for their young person.

In this chapter, we have talked about the different ways children and adolescents exercise faith. Effective Christian parenting requires that we have some knowledge of our child's faith development. In chapters 4 through 6, we will look further at this idea of development, as it relates to the duties of Christian parenting. But first, I want to introduce you to a twofold method of Christian child rearing, proposed through the preaching and writings of John Wesley.

DISCUSSION QUESTIONS

1. Write out and/or discuss the changes in your faith exercise at the beginning of the chapter.

2. Discuss the statement: "God has created each of us with perceptions or understandings that unfold gradually and in orderly fashion throughout life, in matters of faith and morality."

3. How does the concept of faith development relate to Christian child rearing?

4. What are some characteristics of:
   a. stage one faith?
   b. stage two faith?
   c. stage three faith?

5. Can you relate instances where you observed these characteristics in your own children?

6. Discuss Westerhoff's concepts of "dependent" faith and "searching" faith as they relate to teens.

3

J. W. and the Kids

Question: "What is the best way to read a book?" Answer: "The best way to read a book is from beginning to end." That is generally the rule, and this book is no exception. While this chapter contains material that is historical in nature, it is nonetheless invaluable for understanding the rest of the book and child rearing in general. Though many of the experiences are drawn from a couple of centuries ago, they are by no means church history as such (which may or may not be your thing). Rather, the accounts include principles that are both timeless and timely.

Child Rearing in 18th-Century England

If we do not understand a little about child rearing in the era in which John Wesley grew up, we are not likely to understand and appreciate his views. In chapter 1 it was mentioned that the 18th century had a very limited understanding of childhood. Wesley and the early Methodists were no exception. There were cases of harsh discipline and strict regimentation, but the alternatives were even more appalling. Children as young as five years were employed to work in mines or as chimney sweeps, crawling slowly to what was for some an early death in a world of darkness. In the wake of the industrial revolution, many were transported from cities to work in the mills. Again, some died prematurely due to the poor working conditions.[1] This gives us an idea of the value

English society placed on child life in those days. Wesley and the early Methodists made their mistakes, but they loved and valued children, and to suggest otherwise is simply not true.[2]

Although it varied from class to class and from family to family, a change in accepted child-rearing theory and practice took place in England between 1660 and 1800. Children began being treated more affectionately. In fact, there were six styles of parenting practiced by 1800. I'll not comment on each, but they ranged from the "negligent" and "permissive" styles of the well-to-do to the "brutal" and "indifferent" styles of the poor. The child-rearing style of the Wesleys—practiced by mother Susanna and advocated by her childless son John—fell in between these two extremes. By 18th-century standards, they would have been considered moderates. They were not so rich that they would not devote much time to children, or so poor that they could not.[3]

Susanna Wesley: Model Christian Parent

A few years ago I developed a Mother's Day sermon from Prov. 31:10-31, where the writer honors the virtuous woman. Read the last six verses from that chapter (NIV):

> She speaks with wisdom, and faithful instruction is on her tongue. She watches over the affairs of her household and does not eat the bread of idleness. Her children arise and call her blessed; her husband also, and he praises her: "Many women do noble things, but you surpass them all." Charm is deceptive, and beauty is fleeting; but a woman who fears the Lord is to be praised. Give her the reward she has earned, and let her works bring her praise at the city gate.

The preparation and delivery of that sermon was not without its difficulties. At the time, my mother had cancer and was not expected to live. Two months later she graduated to the Church Triumphant. In the sermon I told how, as a boy,

I would sometimes burst into my mother's room without knocking. Often I would find her on her knees praying beside the bed. I reminded her of this in a letter just a couple of months before she died. I told her that God surely used such scenes—scenes of a praying mother—to influence me in my lifework. This is not to idealize her now that she's gone. Mother was far from perfect, and no one knew that better than she. Her favorite word of self-description was "nervous," and she was that. Still, there was a spiritual sensitivity about her that made a deep impression on me. Thank God for Christian mothers—and the resurrection to come!

There was one other mother who was described that day in the sermon. She was the epitome of the virtuous woman described in Proverbs 31. Her name was Susanna Wesley, mother of John Wesley. She ranks among the greatest of Christian parents. Devoted wife of Samuel Wesley and mother of her two famous sons, John and Charles, she gave birth to 19 children, 10 of whom survived infancy. She gave more than careful attention to the spiritual and educational needs of her children. It is difficult, if not impossible, to talk about the child-rearing methods of John Wesley without discussing his mother, Susanna.

You would think that with all of her children, she would have had time only for their physical needs. Yet she personally gave each of her children thorough spiritual training. Every week she made time to talk with each child about spiritual matters. In a letter to her minister-husband, Samuel, who was often away from home on church business, she explains how she began setting aside special times for each child's spiritual nurture. "I take such a proportion of time as I can spare every night, to discourse with each child apart. On Monday, I talk with Molly; on Tuesday, with Hetty; Wednesday, with Nancy; Thursday, with Jacky [John]; Friday, with Patty; Saturday, with Charles; and with Emily and Suky on Sunday."[4]

These weekly sessions with their mother left an impression on the minds of the children, particularly John. Did you notice which night was John's? It was Thursday night. Thursday evenings became special to John Wesley for the rest of his life. We know this from a letter he wrote her years later, as a young man. He was asking her to pray for him during that same time they used to spend together on Thursday evenings.

> In many things you have interceded for me and prevailed. Who knows but in this too you may be successful? If you can spare me only that little part of Thursday evening, which you formerly bestowed upon me in another manner, I doubt not but it would be as useful now for correcting my heart, as it was then for forming my judgment.[5]

Why did Susanna do this? Why did she make time for each child every week? It's not like she didn't have anything else to do. Actually, she did it because she looked upon each one of her children as "talents," committed to her care by God. She explains this in a letter to Samuel again.

> And if I am unfaithful to him or you, in neglecting to improve these talents, how shall I answer unto him, when he shall command me to render an account of my stewardship? . . . These, and other such like thoughts, made me at first take a more than ordinary care of the souls of my children.[6]

Have you ever thought of your children as "talents"? Susanna no doubt had in mind Jesus' parable of the talents in Matt. 25:14-30. In the parable, a man set out on a long journey. Before he left, he called three of his servants together and entrusted his property to them. To one he gave five talents of money; to the second, two talents; and to the third, one talent. A talent was worth more than $1,000. When the owner returned, he found that the servants with the five and two talents had invested their money and earned more. They were both commended. The third servant had not done anything with his one talent and was condemned.

Susanna Wesley understood that her children were not hers at all but God's. They had simply been committed into her keeping for a while. One day she would have to account to God for what she had done with those children. Perhaps if more of us looked upon our children as Susanna did hers, we would say with her, "[This] made me . . . take a more than ordinary care of the souls of my children."

To give an indication of Susanna's influence on John, her method of child rearing is primarily preserved in a lengthy letter she wrote to him at his request, dated July 24, 1732. In it Susanna talked about the management of her children's wills. John used this section with few changes in his sermon titled "On Obedience to Parents." In fact, he used ideas and wording from other parts of this one letter in all of his sermons relating to children.[7]

Susanna believed that the most important factor in a child's spiritual development was obedience. This meant conquering the child's will as soon as possible. Self-will, believed Susanna, was the root of all sin. Once the will was subdued, there would be fewer difficulties in teaching. Parents who understood and practiced this, she regarded as coworkers with God. Parents who did not understand and practice this, she regarded as coworkers with the devil.[8] To Susanna, conquering the will meant primarily "a refusal to let the child have its own way," not breaking the child's spirit. The fact that John asked for his mother's method of child rearing shows that he was not alienated by it.[9]

Susanna's conquering of the will was joined by a disciplining of the mind. As soon as her children reached their fifth birthday, school was conducted in the home for six hours a day—from nine o'clock to twelve and from two to five. Schoolwork consisted of reading, writing, and religion.

On one occasion her husband, Samuel, sat in on one of the sessions and counted the number of times she repeated one bit of information to the same child. Later John recalled, "I remember to have heard my father asking my mother, 'How could you have the patience to tell that blockhead the same thing twenty times over?' She answered, 'Why, if I had told him but nineteen times, I should have lost all my labour.' What patience indeed, what love, what knowledge is requisite for this."[10]

Susanna closed her letter to John with eight rules or "by-laws" that constituted a kind of children's charter in her home. First, to prevent lying for fear of punishment, if a child confessed his fault and promised not to do it again, he would not be beaten. Second, no sinful action would ever remain unpunished. Third, no child would ever be scolded or beaten twice for the same fault. If they did not do it again, they would never be reminded of it. Fourth, every act of obedience would be praised and often rewarded by genuine affection. Fifth, if a child's intentions were good, though not his performance, recognition and instruction on how to accomplish the task would be given. Sixth, the rights and possessions of others must be honored. Seventh, promises must be kept and gifts not taken back unless agreed upon otherwise. Eighth, "no girl be taught to work till she can read very well; and then that she be kept to her work with the same application, and for the same time, that she was held to in reading."[11] This is why Susanna's daughters could read far better than the average woman in 18th-century England.

There is so much more that could be written about Susanna Wesley, but this should give you an idea of the kind of Christian parent she was. The influence she had over her children was powerful and lasting. This influence is felt by us today through the preaching and hymn writing of her sons, John and Charles.

John's Twofold Method

John Wesley understood Christian child rearing to be a twofold task: discipline and instruction. We see this in his sermon "On Family Religion," taken from Josh. 24:15: "As for me and my house, we will serve the Lord."[12] This implies that he believed the fathers should take an active, if not leading, role in Christian child rearing. He further urged parents to see their children as "immortal spirits," whom God has committed to their care for a brief time. He added, "Every child, therefore, you are to watch over with the utmost care, that, when you are called to give an account of each to the Father . . . , you may give your accounts with joy and not with grief."[13] This sounds very similar to Susanna's talk about "talents," doesn't it? Both of them believed that children belonged to God and that parents were responsible for how they raised their children.

Wesley's twofold method of Christian child rearing is spelled out here.

> May we not endeavour, First, to *restrain* them from all outward sin . . . Your children, while they are young, you may restrain from evil, not only by advice, persuasion, and reproof, but also by *correction*; only remembering, that this means is to be used last . . . And even then you should take the utmost care to avoid the very appearance of passion. . . . May we not endeavour, Secondly, to *instruct* them? to take care that every person who is under our roof have all such knowledge as is necessary to salvation?[14]

Let's look at each one of these methods separately and see what John Wesley really did believe about them.

Discipline

In addition to his sermon "On Family Religion," Wesley preached another sermon that tells us a lot about his understanding of discipline. The sermon is titled "On the Education of Children," and the text is drawn from Prov. 22:6: "Train up a child in the way he should go: and when he is old, he will not depart from it."[15] Wesley cautioned parents against taking this verse in its absolute sense—as if no child that had ever been trained in the way he should go had ever departed from it. "It has been a common observation, 'Some of the best parents have the worst children,'" Wesley preached.[16] That's encouraging to hear, isn't it, parents? Still, Wesley believed that the most probable way for making Christians is by raising them, as his text indicates.

The sermon asks two basic questions: "What is 'the way wherein a child should go?' and how shall we 'train him up' therein?"[17] These two questions sound very much like the two headings in "The Family Blueprint: My Design for Disciple Making" in chapter 1: "What Do I Want My Child to Become?" and "How Can I Seek to Make That Happen?" "What?" and "How?" These are two important questions for Christian parents. Wesley's first question implies a theology of discipline, and his second question raises the issue of disciplinary methods. Let's look at both.

Theology of Discipline

Wesley's theological understanding of discipline was basically twofold also: to teach children obedience to parents when the parents' will seemed, to the children, to be the will of God; and to correct the sinful bias of human nature, particularly self-will. Wesley did not believe that human nature would unfold positively without discipline.

The most important work of discipline, believed Wesley, was to cure the disease of self-will. Like his mother, he believed self-will to be the root of all sin. So he strongly urged parents not to let their children have their own willful ways. If children were allowed to have their own ways, they would never learn to obey parents or God. The way to teach this obedience, thought Wesley, was to break their wills as early as possible. Wesley is notorious for his will-breaking statements, but they sounded a lot worse than they really were. He meant primarily a refusal to let children have their own willful ways. As far as Wesley was concerned, there was nothing more important than this in all of Christian education. If children learned to obey their parents, they would be ready to obey God when they were grown.[18]

Wesley talked about this further in another one of his sermons, "On Obedience to Parents." He selected his text from Col. 3:20, where children are commanded to obey their parents. In the sermon, Wesley emphasized the authority of parents. He said, "God has given a power to parents, which even sovereign princes have not. . . . The will of the parent is a law to the child, who is bound in conscience to submit thereto, unless it be contrary to the law of God."[19]

Wesley blamed parents for not understanding the need to break the will of a child. He described a scene where a parent tells a child to do something and the child replies, "I won't!" Wesley believed that such behavior, overlooked by parents, would result in rebellion against God. He urged parents to take immediate action, until the child is "thoroughly afraid ever of giving that diabolical answer again."

> Stop him, stop him at first, in the name of God. Do not "spare the rod, and spoil the child." If you have not the heart of a tiger, do not give up your child to his own will, that is, to the devil. . . . Make them submit, that they may not perish. Break their wills, that you may save their soul.[20]

Wesley did not consider it impossible to break the wills of older children—8 or 10—just far more difficult. He considered this difficulty for the parents "just reward" for past neglect on their part.[21]

Perhaps Wesley's most interesting and important document on discipline is an article he wrote titled "A Thought on the Manner of Educating Children." It shows that he strongly disliked extremism in discipline—unnecessary punishment on the one hand and permissiveness on the other.

> If [parents] either give children too much of their own will, or needlessly and churlishly restrain them; if they either use no punishment at all, or more than is necessary, the leaning either to one extreme or the other may frustrate all their endeavours. In the latter case, it will not be strange if religion stink in the nostrils of those that were so educated. They will naturally look upon it as an austere, melancholy thing; and if they think it necessary to salvation, they will esteem it a necessary evil, and so put it off as long as possible.[22]

Wesley believed that parents should administer discipline with "mildness, softness, and gentleness." If such methods failed to work, then, and only then, "we must correct with kind severity," he declared.[23]

Methods of Discipline

Although Wesley urged parents to break the wills of their children, very little is ever said on how to accomplish it. The "rod" was the enduring symbol of discipline in the 18th century (and Wesley certainly advocated its use, as you've probably noticed), but its use was probably exaggerated and the least effective means of discipline. Discipline tended to be as much psychological as physical.[24] For example, Wesley warned parents against giving children what they cried for. He said:

> There is one advice, which, though little known, should be particularly attended to. It may seem a small circumstance; but it is of more consequence than one can easily imagine. It is this: Never, on any account, give a child any thing that it cries for. For it is a true observation, (and you may make the experiment as often as you please,) if you give a child what he cries for, you pay him for crying; and then he will certainly cry again.[25]

49

To the objection, "But . . . he will scream all day long," Wesley responded, "No mother need suffer a child to cry aloud after it is a year old." He used his own mother and her 10 children as an example, who were said never to be heard crying after a year old.[26]

Wesley also advised parents to praise children sparingly, lest they encourage sinful pride.

> If you ask, "But how shall I encourage them when they do well, if I am never to commend them?" I answer, I did not affirm this; I did not say, "You are *never* to commend them." . . . But I say, use it . . . sparingly; and when you use it, let it be with the utmost caution, directing them, at the same moment, to look upon all they have as the free gift of God.[27]

Still another example of Wesley's discipline included restrictions upon food, eating habits, clothing, and toys. He warned parents against giving children "pretty playthings, glittering toys, shining buckles or buttons, fine clothes, red shoes, laced hats, needless ornaments, as ribands, necklaces, ruffles; yea, and by proposing any of these as *rewards* for doing their duty, which is stamping a great value upon them."[28] Wesley believed that to give children such things encouraged their love for this world and lessened their love for God.

We might raise our eyebrows and call these ideas of Wesley "eccentricities," particularly the one about clothing and toys; but it is an interesting contrast to the materialistic society in which our sons and daughters are growing up today. Don't you agree?

Instruction

The second task in Wesley's twofold method of Christian child rearing was instruction. In a letter he once wrote to a Miss Bishop, he first quoted Mr. Baxter: "'Whoever attempt[s] to teach children will find need of all the understanding God has given them.' But indeed natural understanding will go but a little way. It is a peculiar gift of God."[29] Perhaps this would be a good stopping place to bow our heads, right now, and ask God to supply what we lack as teachers of our children.

O God, when I compare all the responsibilities of Christian parenting with my strength and abilities, I feel overwhelmed and discouraged. Please help me! Give me strength and abilities equal to my tasks. Use me to influence for You the "talent(s)" You have committed into my keeping. I pray this in Jesus' name. Amen.

In his sermon "On Family Religion," Wesley gave parents his guiding principle of teaching in this compact sentence: "You should particularly endeavour to instruct your children, early, plainly, frequently, and patiently."[30] Let's look briefly at each one of these four principles of instruction.

Early Instruction

Wesley believed that instruction should begin as early in life as possible. "Instruct [children] early, from the first hour that you perceive reason begins to dawn. Truth may then begin to shine upon the mind far earlier than we are apt to suppose. . . . Whenever a child begins to speak, you may be assured reason begins to work."[31] Wesley realized that young children were limited in their ability to understand. For example, he recalled with fondness the early instruction he received from Susanna, but admitted, "All that was said to me of inward obedience or holiness I neither understood nor remembered."[32] Still, Wesley did not know of any reason why parents should not begin speaking of the best things—the things of God—as early as possible.

Plain Instruction

In his second principle of "plain" instruction, Wesley urged parents to "use such words as little children may understand, just such as they use themselves. Carefully observe the few ideas which they have already, and endeavour to graft what you say upon them."[33] Wesley practiced what he preached at this point, too. He once promised to preach a sermon to children using no word over two syllables. He later fulfilled this promise to a group of 550 Methodist Sunday School children. He preached from the text, "Come, ye children, hearken unto me [and] I will teach you the fear of the Lord" (Ps. 34:11).[34]

Wesley did not believe that parents should allow children to leave a subject until they thoroughly understood it. "Above all, let them not read nor say one line without understanding and minding what they say. Try them over and over; stop them short, almost in every sentence, and ask them, 'What do you mean by that? Read it again.' So that, if it be possible, they may pass nothing till it has taken hold upon them."[35]

Frequent Instruction

Wesley believed that the soul should be fed no less often than the body. "It would be of little or no service to [instruct children] only once or twice a week. How often do you feed their bodies? Not less than three times a day. And is the soul of less value than the body? Will you not then feed this as often?"[36] He urged parents to say something about God throughout the day, instead of talking strictly about other things.

Patient Instruction

Wesley felt that parents should never give up on their children, that parents' efforts should not stop until they can see the fruit of their labors. To do this, he believed parents had to pray for perseverance as a gift from God. For parents who had yet to see any results in their children, Wesley urged unceasing prayer.[37]

In addition to his four principles of instruction, John Wesley understood instruction to be both formal and informal. Let's look at both of them.

Formal Instruction

To assist parents, as well as preachers and schoolmasters, in the religious education of the young, Wesley prepared several textbooks and tracts. A study of these resources suggests three essentials of religious instruction: Scripture, prayer, and music.

Scripture. John Wesley believed that children should learn the Bible! It was his focal point for teaching them the truths about God. Among the tracts and textbooks he prepared to help children learn the Bible, his *Lessons for Children* and *Instructions for Children* were the most important. His *Lessons for Children* was a series of 200 Bible studies for children, all based on the Old Testament. His *Instructions for Children* consisted of 58 lessons for children, covering a variety of biblical subjects. Of the two, Wesley gave the *Instructions* chief place among textbooks for children in the home.[38] In his words, "The 'Instructions for Children' contain the best matter that we can possibly teach them. But nothing less than the finger of God can write it on their hearts."[39] We would do well to remember that last piece of advice in teaching our own children God's Word.

The prefaces to both the *Lessons* and *Instructions* were addressed "To All Parents and Schoolmasters." It would be helpful to read a part of the preface to the *Lessons,* because it tells us something about Wesley's method of teaching children. He urged parents to ask questions.

> I cannot but earnestly entreat you to take good heed, how you teach these deep things of God. Beware of that

common, but accursed way of making children parrots, instead of Christians. Labour that, as far as possible, they may understand every single sentence which they read. Therefore, do not make haste. Regard not how much but how well, or of how good purpose, they read. Turn each sentence every way, propose it in every light, and question them continually on every point; if by any means they may not only read, but inwardly digest the words of eternal life.[40]

Prayer. The second essential of religious instruction was prayer. Wesley believed that children should not only be taught to pray, but how to pray. He even prepared several forms of prayer for teaching them. His *Prayers for Children* gave a brief prayer for the morning and evening of each day, a short prayer for family and friends, and two "graces" for before and after meals.[41]

Music. Wesley used music as a third essential for teaching children. His *Hymns for Children* was one of his last publications, published in 1790, one year before his death. It shows his concern for children even in his old age.[42]

Wesley's method of formal instruction was to meet with children separately, but it was also for parents to meet with children for family worship. He recommended family worship for both morning and evening, and it included all three of his essentials of religious instruction: Scripture, prayer, and music. Wesley even prepared an order of service to assist parents.

A short prayer was offered at the opening, then a psalm sung, and the Scriptures read and expounded. This done, the children were required to give some account of what they had heard, whereupon the meaning of it was further fixed in their minds by their parents. A longer prayer followed. The worship concluded with a benediction or the doxology. Before the family separated, the children would ask a blessing of their parents, which was invariably given.[43]

54

Informal Instruction

Besides the somewhat formal times of instruction, Wesley advised parents to use the opportunities that came from the routine of everyday life. In his sermon "On Family Religion," he pictured a parent using the sun to illustrate God's love.

> Bid the child look up; and ask, "What do you see there?" "The sun." "See, how bright it is! Feel how warm it shines upon your hand! Look, how it makes the grass and the flowers to grow, and the trees and everything look green! But God, though you cannot see him, is above the sky, and is a deal brighter than the sun! It is he, it is God that made the sun, and you, and me, and everything. It is he that makes the grass and the flowers grow; that makes the trees green, and the fruit to come upon them! Think what he can do! He can do whatever he pleases. . . . he loves you; he loves to do you good. He loves to make you happy."[44]

Wesley told parents to pray that God would use such opportunities to teach children. This one illustration is enough to know that Wesley did not limit teaching to the more formal times of instruction.

It is obvious that John Wesley was very concerned about the religious education of the young. He not only urged parents to implement Christian education in the home, but he provided them the resources to do so. In the remaining chapters of this book, we're going to see how Wesley's twofold method of Christian child rearing—discipline and instruction—can help us as Christian parents today.

DISCUSSION QUESTIONS

1. How did Wesley understand Christian child rearing?

2. Susanna Wesley viewed her children as "talents." John Wesley saw children as "immortal spirits." What significance do these concepts have for Christian parenting?

3. Read Prov. 22:6. Discuss Wesley's thoughts on this verse, particularly his statement: "Some of the best parents have the worst children."

4. What role did discipline play in Wesley's understanding of Christian child rearing?

5. Discuss:
    a. Wesley's "four principles" for teaching children
    b. Wesley's "three essentials" for teaching children
    c. Wesley's formal vs. informal instruction

4

Stop That Child!
(Discipline)

Picture yourself driving across town. You're making excellent time because you've hit several green lights just right. As you approach the next intersection, the light suddenly turns yellow, so you proceed through it with caution. Finally, the inevitable happens. The next stoplight turns red before you reach it, and you have to apply your brakes to stop.

I want you to picture your children's behavior as a stoplight. There is "green" behavior, "yellow" behavior, and "red" behavior. Green means behavior that you like or desire in your children. It is behavior to which you say yes. Yellow means behavior that you tolerate in your children for special reasons. For example, their behavior may not be the most desirable because they're learning something new, or maybe they're not feeling well. Red means behavior that you do not like in your children and will not tolerate under any circumstances. It is behavior to which you say no. It may mean behavior that endangers the children or others, behavior that infringes upon the rights of others, behavior that goes beyond the rules, or maybe behavior that is clearly in defiance of your authority as a parent.

Now that we've identified these "three zones of discipline,"[1] take out a sheet of paper and write down some examples of one of your children's behavior. Your paper might look something like this:

"Green" behavior

1. She says, "Please," and "Thank you."
2. She cleans up her room every night.
3. Etcetera.

"Yellow" behavior

1. She is slow getting ready for school.
2. She forgets to put away her bicycle.
3. Etcetera.

"Red" behavior

1. She says, "Shut up!"
2. She hits the neighbor girl.
3. Etcetera.

This exercise is a good way to start us thinking about discipline. Once we have identified our children's behavior, we can work on either strengthening it or changing it. This exercise also tells us that children need a clear definition of acceptable and unacceptable behavior. They need to know what is expected of them.[2]

Before we barge right into a discussion on methods of discipline, we should think about a theology of discipline, as John Wesley taught us. In other words, before we look at the "how" of discipline, we need to look at the "what," or maybe the "why," of discipline. Why should we, as Christian parents, discipline our children?

Theology of Discipline

We learned in chapter 3 that Wesley's theological understanding of discipline was twofold: to correct the sinful bias of human nature, particularly self-will; and to teach children obedience to parents, when the parents' will seemed to the children to be the will of God. Let's think about each one of these briefly.

First, discipline is to correct the sinful bias of human

nature, particularly self-will. Child psychologist James Dobson sounds very much like Wesley when he recommends that we "shape the will while preserving the spirit" of children "intact." Spirit, as Dobson defines it, "relates to the self-esteem or the personal worth that a child feels." Parents shape the will and preserve the spirit, writes Dobson, "by establishing reasonable boundaries and enforcing them with love, but by avoiding any implication that the child is unwanted, unnecessary, foolish, ugly, dumb, a burden, an embarrassment, or a disastrous mistake."[3]

A word of caution is in order. The willfulness of early childhood should not be automatically regarded by parents as defiance to be conquered. The time young children spend preoccupied with themselves creates a sense of uniqueness and separateness. In order for children to become morally responsible, they must become self-conscious, then God-conscious, and finally choice-conscious. Independence marks the beginning of wise judgment, discernment, and inner conviction, which are all characteristics of mature Christianity.[4] This is not to minimize the need for firm parental control or deny that real battles of will do sometimes occur between parents and their children. Rather, it is recognizing that self-centeredness, sometimes manifesting itself negatively in a child, is considered by many as a normal part of development. Sometimes the child's protests are little more than playacting designed to find out how it feels to say no. The parent who continues unperturbed to dress the child or tuck him into bed may find the child still cooperating through a refrain of verbal resistance. If a parent fails to detect the playful quality of a child's negativism, an actual crisis of authority may occur where none existed before.[5] So, shape the will? By all means! Break their spirit? Absolutely not!

Not only is discipline to correct the sinful bias of human nature, particularly that of self-will, but also it is to teach children obedience. Dobson again sounds very much like

Wesley, who believed that children learn to obey God when they learn to obey their parents. Listen to Dobson.

> By learning to yield to the loving authority (leadership) of his parents, a child learns to submit to other forms of authority which will confront him later in life. The way he sees his parents' leadership sets the tone for his eventual relationships with his teachers, school principal, police, neighbors, and employers. . . .
>
> There is an even more important reason for the preservation of authority in the home: *while yielding to the loving leadership of their parents, children are also learning to yield to the benevolent leadership of God Himself.* It is a well known fact that a child identifies his parents with God, whether the adults want that role or not *(italics added)*.[6]

Did you get that? *Children learn to obey God when they learn to obey their parents!* This is particularly true for young children. Remember our discussion about stage one faith in chapter 2? It is difficult for stage one children (two or three years old to six or seven years old) to say where Mom and Dad stop and God begins. They identify their parents with God. This mean that early childhood is a prime period for the teaching of obedience through discipline.

Discipline as Teaching

Let's play a little word-association game. What is the first thing that comes to your mind when you hear the word *discipline?* Many people associate the word *discipline* with punishment. This is unfortunate, because *discipline* means *teaching!* Discipline is not something prior to or outside the learning process, it *is* the learning process itself. Or more precisely, it is a way in which learning takes place. The word *discipline* comes from the Latin verb *discere,* meaning "to learn."[7] When parents are faced with a disciplinary encounter, they are confronted by the question, "What will my child *learn* from this experience?" If the goal is to teach, then parents should know what they are wanting to teach.[8] Often, parents think only in terms of punishment. They do this for two reasons: (1) a parent tends to discipline in the manner he was disciplined as a child, and (2) finding alternatives to punishment requires more personal effort and creativity than most parents are willing to give. It is much easier to use the same disciplinary method for every situation; spanking, for example. This is unfortunate, since by role definition, a *parent* is supposed to be a *teacher!*

Interestingly, not only does the word *discipline* come from the Latin verb *discere,* but so does the word *disciple.*[9] The following diagram illustrates what I'm talking about.

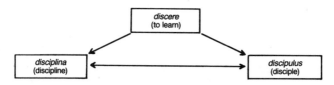

Notice how the word *discipline* is related to the word *disciple.* When parents, as teachers, discipline their children, they are teaching them to be their disciples. Did you catch that? *Parents make disciples when they discipline their children!* This is to say, it is only when discipline becomes self-discipline that children can become disciples. You see, the purpose of discipline is to teach children to do the right thing and to help them develop the inner motivation to continue doing so. Punishment can enforce obedience, but obedience is not the only goal in parent-child relations. It is but a first step. Self-control and self-discipline should be the eventual goals sought. So, to repeat, it is only when discipline becomes self-discipline that children can become disciples.[10]

Psychologist Martin L. Hoffman points out that this whole business of self-discipline begins with the disciplinary methods used by parents. As parents discipline their kids, says Hoffman, children gradually learn to control their own "egoistic, self-serving motives."[11] This sounds very much like Wesley and his talk about "self-will," doesn't it? Let's turn our attention now from a theology of discipline to methods of discipline.

Methods of Discipline

Please understand that I do not consider myself an expert when it comes to child discipline—neither in theory nor in practice. Rather, I consider myself very much a tourist in a strange, unpredictable land. There are, however, some things that have been learned about discipline that have helped me as a Christian parent. These are some of the things to be shared in the remainder of this chapter. Consider it an introduction or overview to several different, developmental strategies of discipline. You might want to pull out that "three zones of discipline" exercise and keep it close by for reference. Let's begin by talking about the "trinity of discipline."

The Trinity of Discipline

Discipline consists basically of three things: structure, intervention, and consistency. The following diagram will help us picture this.

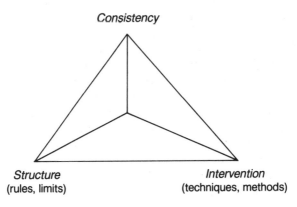

Structure refers to the overall rules and limits to a child's world. Think back to the "three zones of discipline" exercise at the beginning of the chapter. That exercise helped us establish rules and limits to our children's behavior ("red" behavior). We know that one of our most basic needs, as human beings, is the physical and psychological need for safety or security. This need for safety or security is best provided for children in a world that has routine, consistency, and proper authority. Without clearly understood rules and limits, children will often seek security through misbehavior. Whether children hate the rules that go against them or love the rules that help them, the fact is, *children desperately need rules and limits!* Structure does not mean a rigidly enforced schedule. It means a fairly predictable world, where children can have some idea of their routine and can know the limits of acceptable behavior.

Intervention refers to the successful maintenance of this structure through the various techniques, strategies, or methods of discipline. This is what we're about to discuss.

Consistency—well, you understand how important consistency is in anything. To discipline undesirable behavior one moment but not the next not only confuses the child but also undermines parental authority. It tells the child that parents can be pushed.

Structure, intervention, and consistency describe how the system of discipline works, but things like love, thoughtfulness, and patience really make it successful.[12] As we look at some of the strategies of discipline, let us not forget that they are but a part of the overall "trinity of discipline."

Disciplinary strategies can be divided into two groups: strategies that focus on communicating feelings, and strategies that focus on changing behavior.[13] This says that there is no *one* approach to discipline.

Strategies That Focus on Communicating Feelings

The "three zones of discipline" exercise told us that children need to know what is expected of them. This means that *parents should always use communication as their first method of discipline!* Verbal communication can sometimes prevent misbehavior. There are a couple of strategies, I think, that illustrate well this communication of feelings between parents and children. The first is proposed by psychologist Thomas Gordon, with his techniques of "active listening" and "I messages"; and the second is proposed by physician Spencer Johnson—his techniques are the "one minute reprimands," "one minute praisings," and "one minute goals." Let's overview Gordon's strategy first.

Active Listening

Thomas Gordon's technique of "active listening" is designed to facilitate communication between parent and child, when the child "owns the problem" (has the problem), but the parent does not. Active listening is basically "feedback." Parents listen carefully to what the child is saying, then feed back their understanding of the child's feelings in words similar to the child's statement. Such listening allows the child to get rid of negative feelings either causing or surrounding the problem. It also demonstrates to the child the parents' love and acceptance.

Gordon gives the following example of active listening:

Child: Tommy won't play with me today. He won't ever do what I want to do.

Parent: You're kinda angry with Tommy *(active listening)*.

Child: I sure am. I never want to play with him again. I don't want him for a friend.

Parent: You're so angry you feel like never seeing him again *(active listening)*.

Child: That's right. But if I don't have him for a friend, I won't have anyone to play with then.

Parent: You would hate to be left with no one *(active listening).*

Child: Yeah. I guess I just have to get along with him someway. But it's so hard for me to stop getting mad at him.

Parent: You want to get along better but it's hard for you to keep from getting mad with Tommy *(active listening).*

Child: I never used to—but that's when he was always willing to do what I wanted to do. He won't let me boss him anymore.

Parent: Tommy's not so easy to influence now *(active listening).*

Child: He sure isn't. He's not such a baby now. He's more fun though.

Parent: You really like him better this way *(active listening).*

Child: Yeah. But it's hard to stop bossing him—I'm so used to it. Maybe we wouldn't fight so much if I let him have his way once in a while. Think that would work?

Parent: You're thinking that you might give in occasionally; it might help *(active listening).*

Child: Yeah, maybe it would. I'll try it.

It is apparent from this conversation that the parent, using active listening, is trying to encourage the child to express his feelings as well as find a solution to the problem. All of us can relate to the good feeling of really being heard by someone else and understood. Children are no different. They have feelings, too! Gordon warns that active listening is not merely parroting or repeating the child's own words, either. It is feeding back your understanding of the child's feelings in words similar to the child's own words. In the following example notice the difference between parroting and feedback.

Child: I never get a chance to get the ball when the bigger kids start playing catch.

Parent (a): You never get a chance to get the ball with big kids *(parroting)*.

Parent (b): You want to play, too, and you feel it's not fair for them to leave you out *(feeding back the meaning)*. [14]

The essence of this feedback technique is basically three-fold: (1) listening carefully to what your child is saying; (2) formulating in your mind what your child is expressing; and (3) feeding back to him the feelings he has just expressed to you. [15]

I Messages

Gordon's second technique is called "I messages" and is designed to facilitate communication between parent and child when the parent "owns the problem" (has the problem), but the child does not. For example, many parents of teenagers find themselves very upset at their son's or daughter's messy room, but the teenager does not seem to mind at all. When this happens, it is the parent who must communicate feelings and frustrations to the child. Gordon tells parents to use "I messages" and *not* "you messages" (like "You slowpoke!"), because "you messages" tend to be judgmental, which hurts the child's self-esteem. [16]

"I messages" consist basically of three parts: (1) a clear statement of how the parent feels; (2) the child's behavior that caused the parent to feel that way; and (3) why the behavior is upsetting to the parent. For example, a parent who is upset with a teenager's messy room might say, "I feel upset and frustrated when I look at your messy room, because the family works hard to make the house look clean and neat, and your room spoils all our efforts." [17]

Let's move now from Thomas Gordon to Spencer Johnson. Johnson's is a three-part communication method that takes only about a minute or so for each part. It consists of "one minute reprimands," "one minute praisings," and "one minute goals."

One Minute Reprimands

The key to "one minute reprimands" is to remember that a child's behavior may not be OK, but the child is OK! In other words, the parent wants the child to feel bad about his misbehavior but good about himself. The reprimand is divided into two parts. In the first part, the child is reprimanded immediately after the misbehavior occurs. The child is told specifically what he did and how it makes the parent feel. Then, for a few unpleasant seconds, the parent is silent to let the child feel what the parent is feeling. For example, the parent says, *I am upset! I am very upset!* and then lets that sink in for a few unpleasant moments. In the second half of the reprimand, the parent calms down and touches the child to convey love and confidence. The parent reminds the child that while the behavior was not good, he is good. The child is then given a hug and told, "I love you!" Once the reprimand is over, it's over. The incident is not mentioned again.

One Minute Praisings

While a one minute reprimand is corrective discipline, a "one minute praising" is preventive discipline. One minute praisings are designed to prevent misbehavior by catching children in the act of doing something right. This, in turn, strengthens desirable behavior, says Johnson.[18] Psychologist Fitzhugh Dodson claims that parents often ignore their child's desirable behavior (such as playing cooperatively with other children) but give prompt attention to undesirable behavior. When this happens, the negative behavior is strengthened. Thus parents violate what Dodson calls the "law of the soggy potato chip." A child obviously prefers a fresh potato chip to a soggy one. But if the choice is between a soggy potato chip and no potato chip, the child will settle for the soggy one. In the same way, a child prefers the parents' positive attention to their negative attention. But if the choice is between negative attention and no attention at all, the child will usually choose the negative attention. For a child—as well as for adults—even negative attention is better than being ignored.[19]

One minute praisings are similar to the second part of the one minute reprimand. Parents catch children in the act of doing something right and tell them specifically what they did and how it makes the parents feel. There is a moment of silence, to let children feel good about themselves, then parents end the praising with a hug or light touch and say, "I love you!"

One Minute Goals

Johnson says that one minute reprimands and praisings emphasize the consequences of children's behavior, but "one minute goals" can *begin* their behavior. He urges parents to help children become more self-disciplined by letting them share in the decision-making process. One way to do this is for family members who are old enough to write down what they would like to see happen as individuals ("I" goals) and as a family ("we" goals). Goals should be specific and written in 250 words or less so that they can be read in about a minute or so. All the participants reread these goals regularly to see if their behavior is matching their goals. The more children review their goals, the greater is the tendency for them to act upon them. Once a week, each person's goals and behavior are reviewed by the entire family to determine progress.[20]

Let's switch our emphasis now from the communication of feelings to strategies that focus on changing behavior.

Strategies That Focus on Changing Behavior

Discipline must be developmental! This means that discipline, to be effective, must fit a child's stage of development. What works with preschoolers will probably not work with teenagers, and vice versa. Let's take the stages of faith development (chap. 2) and see which strategies might work best at each stage.

Infancy/Toddlerhood

Discipline problems do not generally arise during infancy, but *the foundation of discipline is being laid!* Parents have the opportunity to build a deep emotional rapport with the child, which will be the foundation on which discipline rests.

Environmental Control

As the child grows and becomes increasingly mobile, "environmental control" is perhaps the best strategy. This says that fragile adult things should be put away so that the toddler may explore his new world without consequence. If the child's world is filled with untouchables that tempt him into misbehavior, then trouble is sure to follow.[21] James Dob-

---

Stages One and Two Faith (2 or 3 years old to 11 or 12 years old)

Generally speaking, strategies that will work with stage one children (2 or 3 years old to 6 or 7 years old) will also work with stage two children (6 or 7 years old to 11 or 12 years old). Toward the end of stage two, however, parents may find that some of the methods will not work as well.

---

son believes that mild and infrequent spankings can begin during early toddlerhood, but only in defiance of parental authority and never for exploration of the environment.[22]

Natural and Logical Consequences

The strategies of "natural consequences" and "logical consequences" suggest that *children learn when they are allowed to experience the consequences of their behavior.* Natural consequences are those consequences experienced by the child, where there is no interference by parents. Parents stay out of the way and let nature run its course. For example, four-year-old Alice refuses to eat. Daddy prompts her. Alice puts a bite in her mouth but holds it there when Daddy begins talking to Mommy again. Mommy then prompts her. Alice chews vigorously until Mommy and Daddy start talking again. The whole meal is one of continually coaxing Alice to eat. The purpose of Alice's poor appetite is to keep her parents preoccupied with her. The strategy of natural consequences suggests that the simplest way to teach Alice to eat properly is to let her eat. If she refuses, the unfinished food is removed from the table when everyone else is finished. Alice is then allowed to find out what happens: If we don't eat, we get hungry! At the next meal, and not before, food is served. The natural consequences of refusing to eat is hunger!

Logical consequences are similar, except that they are consequences imposed by parents. The parent interferes and structures a plan of consequence that is not naturally there. Take, for example, three-year-old Betty, who doesn't like to brush her teeth. Mommy has to force Betty to brush, and both end up getting upset. Then Mommy thinks of a consequence. Mommy tells Betty that she will not force her to brush her teeth, but that since candy and sweets destroy unbrushed teeth, Betty will not be allowed to have any sweets. No further mention of brushing will be made. For several days, Betty neither brushes her teeth nor has any sweets. One afternoon Betty announces that she wants to brush her teeth and have some candy. Mommy says, "Not now, Betty. Morning is the proper time we brush our teeth." The girl agrees, and the next morning, she brushes her teeth without being told.[23]

Positive Rewards

Let's turn our attention momentarily to the discipline of children where antagonism or confrontation is not necessarily involved. The strategy of "positive rewards" says that when an action or behavior is followed by a reward (or pleasurable consequence), that action or behavior is likely to be repeated. Stated differently, if a child likes what happens as the result of his behavior, he will be inclined to repeat the behavior. With this strategy there is always a reward for desirable behavior, but none for undesirable behavior.

Rewards fall into three general categories: "social rewards," such as attention, approval, praise, and physical affection; "material rewards," such as food or gifts; and "activities and privileges," such as trips, special outings, permission to stay up late, and so on. Of the three types of rewards, it is generally believed that social rewards are the best because they are less costly, less formalized, and have lasting psychological benefits. Within this category, however, individual preferences do exist. Some children enjoy hugs and kisses, while others like verbal compliments. Spencer Johnson's "one minute praisings" are an example of social rewards and how to give them.

Sometimes social rewards alone are not enough. Children may not want to carry out an activity no matter how approving a parent is. In these situations, material rewards, activities, and privileges may be necessary. The following exercise is designed to help us identify those things to which our children are attracted.[24]

Material Rewards

List 10 material rewards, in order, to which your child is attracted. Consider such things as specific toys, foods, drinks, and the like.

1.	6.
2.	7.
3.	8.
4.	9.
5.	10.

List other material rewards that your child does not own, or to which your child does not have ready access, that he would like to have.

1.	4.
2.	5.
3.	6.

Activities and Privileges

List 10 activities, in order, on which your child spends the most time.

1.	6.
2.	7.
3.	8.
4.	9.
5.	10.

List activities or privileges in which you think your child would like to engage more frequently than he does now.

1.   4.

2.   5.

3.   6.

When our daughter, Krista, began attending preschool, she did not want me to leave her in the mornings. Her teacher informed me that she would sometimes cry long after the session began. Neither the teacher nor I felt that her crying was terribly unusual, so one morning Krista and I had a talk. Now you must understand that Krista loved snow cones (and still does, by the way). So I told her we would stop and get a snow cone after school if she wouldn't cry in the mornings. From that moment on the crying stopped, and Krista enjoyed her after-school delight. After a while the snow cones were only offered occasionally, and finally, not at all. Now she can hardly wait to get out of the car and go to school.

Token System

It is important to remember that the faster the rewards are given, the more effective they are. Even though immediate reinforcement is best, sometimes it is not possible. Therefore, "tokens" or a "point system" in the form of a chart or checklist may be necessary. A token system is one in which children earn tokens or points that they can exchange for material rewards, activities, or privileges.[25] James Dobson has developed such a checklist for four- to six-year-olds.[26] I adapted it for use with Krista. Here's what one of her charts looked like.

My Jobs

MARCH	1	2	3	4	5	6	7	8	9	Etc.
1. I minded Daddy today.										
2. I minded Mommy today.										
3. I was nice to Brandon today.										
4. I said, "Please," and "Thank You," today.										
5. I got ready for bed without fussing.										
6. I said my prayers to-night.										
7. I slept in my own bed all last night.										

Each evening before bed, Krista put colored stars beside those behaviors done satisfactorily. Each star represented a penny. If more than two items were missed in a given day, no pennies were given. With this chart, Krista could earn a maximum of 50¢ (rounded off) per week. Every Saturday morning, we did three things with her earnings: We gave her 25¢ to spend as she wished (usually on gum or candy); 10¢ to put in the church offering (she had her own tithing envelopes); and 15¢ to put in a little savings bank. The pennies missed during the week would come out of her spending money. This seemed to provide a little extra incentive. The chart has changed periodically, as certain behaviors have been established and new responsibilities substituted. She has even made suggestions for her revised chart. Periodically, too, we dispense with the chart altogether and start it again at a later time.

There were two immediate and noticeable changes as a result of the chart. One, getting ready for bed, which usually meant taking a bath, ceased to be a big hassle. Two, she began sleeping in her own bed all night (hooray!), which had been an even bigger hassle. And from the use of the chart, Krista learned not only certain behaviors and responsibilities but also good stewardship with her earnings. I have been particularly pleased with the way she makes out her own tithe envelope and gives it in the Sunday School offering. Learning to tithe at such an early age should make tithing quite natural for her later.

Contracting

Whereas a reward or token system works more or less unilaterally—that is, the parent decides which good behavior(s) will be rewarded—"contracting" is based on negotiation. A written contract is negotiated so that the child promises to do a particular thing, and the parent promises to do something in return. Take, for example, 10-year-old Harry and his dad:[27]

> I, Harry Falconer, promise to do the dishes on Monday, Tuesday and Thursday nights. In return for Harry's doing the dishes on those nights, I, Roger Falconer, promise to treat him to anything he wants at the ice cream store.
>
> Signed: _____
> Harry Falconer
>
> _____
> Roger Falconer

Time-out

In the strategy of "time-out," the child is removed from the situation that encourages undesirable behavior. It is basically a cooling-off period—a way of separating a child from

75

a difficult situation and giving him time to calm down. The parent removes the child to a safe but uninteresting area—one where there are no toys or distractions—and insists that the child stay there for a specific period of time. The amount of time depends on the child's age and/or seriousness of the offense.[28] The following steps outline an effective and reasonable use of the time-out method:

1. Decide on a behavior that needs to be changed and explain it to the child. For example, if Jamie hits his sister, explain to Jamie that the hitting must stop.

2. Explain to the child that he will be placed in time-out every time the unacceptable behavior is shown. For example, "You know you can't hit your sister, Jamie. Time out for 5 minutes!"

3. Separate the child from the activity to a place where there are as few people and toys as possible. This does *not* mean that the time-out spot should be uncomfortable or frightening.

4. Decide in advance on how long each time-out will be.

5. Remain calm. Avoid lecturing and getting angry. Simply do the time-out.

6. Tell the child whether he has participated well in time-out. If the child has not been quiet in time-out, start it over again.

7. Use a timer and start with only a few minutes of time-out. Telling a child whose conception of time is unsophisticated that they will have to spend 30 minutes in a chair is unnecessary. Three to 5 minutes will do.

8. Use time-out every time the unacceptable behavior is displayed. Use delayed time-out if the unacceptable behavior occurs while away from home. For example, "You hit your sister, Jamie. You'll need to do a time-out when we get home."

Response Cost

The strategy of "response cost" means just what it says.

Inappropriate behavior costs something! It is basically punishment by loss. For example, a child loses a favorite activity for misbehavior: "no television tonight" or "no outdoor play after dinner" or, with teenagers, "no keys to the car."[29]

Spanking

"Spankings" certainly have their place in discipline, but there are conditions. James Dobson says that spankings do not have the same effect on all children and that spankings should become relatively infrequent during the period immediately prior to adolescence and nonexistent with teenagers altogether.[30] He believes that spankings should be reserved for the moment a child, aged 10 or less, expresses a defiant "I will not!" or "You shut up!" Such behavior, says Dobson (and believed Wesley), represents a direct challenge to parental authority.[31]

Stage Three Faith (adolescence)

Toward the end of stage two (11 or 12 years old), some of the methods we've been discussing will probably not work as well. This includes things like charts and time-outs. This is not to say that such methods will not work with adolescents. This is where parents need to know their children. As a rule, though, *methods that rely on mutual respect rather than the sheer authority of parents tend to appeal more to preadolescents and adolescents!* Methods such as active listening, "I messages," one minute reprimands, one minute praisings, one minute goals, contracting, and response cost tend to work better than some of the others mentioned. Two further strategies that work well with adolescents are "mutual problem-solving" and "family councils."

Mutual Problem-Solving

Psychologist Thomas Gordon outlines six separate steps in the mutual problem-solving or "no-lose" method, as he calls it.

1. Step 1: *Identifying and Defining the Conflict.* Gordon suggests that parents select a time when the child is not busy and tell him clearly and concisely that there is a problem that must be solved. Parents should use "I messages," avoid "you judgments," and find a solution acceptable to both, if possible.

2. Step 2: *Generating Possible Solutions.* The key here is for both parent and child to brainstorm a variety of solutions. "What are some of the things we might do?"

3. Step 3: *Evaluating the Alternative Solutions.* "Now, which of these solutions do we feel is best for us?" Parents should be honest in stating their own feelings when they don't feel comfortable with something.

4. Step 4: *Deciding on the Best Solution.* Gordon says that this step is not as difficult as we might think. Usually, a mutually satisfying decision often surfaces. Solutions should not be set in concrete—say instead, "Let's try this one and see if it works"—and solutions with several points should probably be written down, as in contracting.

5. Step 5: *Implementing the Decision.* Often, after a solution has been reached, there is the need to spell out in detail how it will be implemented—who? what? when? where? how often?

6. Step 6: *Follow-up Evaluation.* Sometimes, solutions turn out to be bad ones. This is why parents should check back with a child to see if he is still happy with it. Sometimes this follow-up requires that the decision be modified.

Gordon believes that communication is the key to mutual problem-solving. Consequently, parents must do a lot of active listening and send clear "I messages." Active listening is necessary because parents need to understand how children feel. "I messages" are needed because children need to understand how parents feel. When a solution cannot be reached in mutual problem-solving, Gordon says to keep talking and generating solutions until one is found that is agreeable.

Family Councils

"Family councils" differ from mutual problem-solving in that mutual problem-solving addresses problems as soon as they occur and does not need to involve the entire family.[32] The family council concept can be thought of as an extension of the mutual problem-solving method. The family council is just what its name implies: a weekly or regular meeting of all family members to make plans, discuss business, and solve problems. Details of the meeting will vary according to each family. For example, some families may choose to meet once a week—say, on Monday evenings—while other families may choose to meet less often. Some families may choose to go 15 minutes or so, while other families may want to meet much longer. Some families may want to have a chairperson and secretary (perhaps on a rotating basis), while others will not want that at all. Whatever the details, all family members should be expected to attend, and each family member should have the right to be heard. Together, all seek for solutions to the problems discussed, à la mutual problem-solving.[33]

Obviously, not everyone agrees on the subject of parental authority. Psychologist Thomas Gordon rejects what he calls "win-lose" methods of discipline (parent wins, child loses; or child wins, parent loses) for a "no-lose" method of resolving family conflicts. In the "no-lose" method, parents and children "possess equal or relatively equal power," says Gordon.[34] Psychologist Rudolf Dreikurs calls for a "democratic atmosphere" in the home and urges parents to sidestep the struggle for power. All family members have an equal voice in the solution of problems. Parents "do not have authority over their children," says Dreikurs.[35]

Were Mr. Wesley alive today, you can no doubt guess what his response might be. Can't we just hear him now? "[Ahem!] God has given a power to parents, which even sovereign princes have not."[36] That may be overstating it a bit, but the message is clear: *Parents do have authority in the home!* Family therapist Salvador Minuchin says it like this: "[Some therapists] mistakenly assume that a democratic society is leaderless, or that a family is a society of peers." He continues, "Effective functioning requires that parents and children accept the fact that [unequal authority] is a necessary ingredient. . . . Children . . . need to know how to negotiate in situations of unequal power."[37] Counselor Howard Clinebell says that the parent-child relationship is not "a relationship of equality." The generation gap "is a necessary and vital phenomenon. Children and adolescents need parents to be parents."[38]

Actually, research on the effects of child-rearing practices on children's behavior lends support to parental authority. Three types of parenting have been identified: authoritative, authoritarian, and permissive. These three types of parents have also been referred to as the "Leader/Guide" parent, the "Boss" parent, and the "Pal" parent, respectively.[39] Findings have shown that the child-rearing practices of authoritative parents enhance the self-esteem of children more than the other two types. "Authoritative parents exercise firm control of the child's behavior, but also emphasize the independence and individuality of the child."[40] In other words, children don't need parents to be bosses, and they don't need parents to be just pals. They need parents to be leaders in the home! The Bible strikes the balance between author-itarianism and permissiveness like this: "Manage [your] own family well and see that [your] children obey [you] with proper respect" (1 Tim. 3:4, NIV), but "do not exasperate your children" (Eph. 6:4, NIV).

DISCUSSION QUESTIONS

1. Write out and/or discuss the "three zones of discipline" exercise at the beginning of the chapter.
2. Discuss the concepts of self-will and obedience as they relate to discipline.
3. Define discipline. What is its relationship to discipleship?
4. What is "the trinity of discipline"?
5. Discuss:
   a. the two disciplinary strategies mentioned that focus on communicating feelings
   b. the disciplinary strategies that focus on changing be-havior
   c. which strategies you have found to be most successful; unsuccessful
6. What is the role of parental authority?

5

Teach Your Children Well

(Formal Instruction)

In her excellent little book *Successful Family Devotions,* Mary White poses a very disturbing question to Christian parents. She asks, "If you knew that your children would never have any other source of spiritual truth other than yourself, would you panic?" I'm getting nervous already! If you think that's bad, listen to her next question. "If all Sunday schools, Christian schools, Christian bookstores, gospel radio and telvision programs, and Christian literature were removed, how would you handle the spiritual training of your family?" Now that's downright terrifying! I mean, how would our little charges learn about God if they couldn't go to Sunday School? Would you like to hear how Mrs. White answers her own questions? OK, but it may not be what you want to hear. "We need to live as though we are the only available source of spiritual training for our children. . . . Many other inputs are excellent, but parents contribute the primary spiritual training in a child's life."[1]

What's your reaction to that? Here's a little test to find out. Is your reaction *(a):* "I know I'm not my child's only source of spiritual training"? Or is it *(b):* "I know I am my child's primary source of spiritual training"? If you responded with *(a),* then chances are you're depending too much on someone else to train up your child in the Christian faith.

The truth is, parents are not the only source of spiritual

training in a child's life, but they are the primary source. We talked about this in chapter 1. Wherever you look in our Judeo-Christian heritage, it is parents who have the primary responsibility for bringing up their children in their particular faith. Other sources of spiritual training, such as the church, do impact the child, but not as much as the parents' training does. Church training, at best, is only an extension or supplement to the training children receive at home from their parents.

Mary White mentioned "panic" as one possibility for Christian parents. It is a thought, but let's refrain for the time being. Instead, let's look again at John Wesley's principles and essentials of formal religious instruction, to see how they can help us become the primary source of spiritual training in our children's lives.

Wesley's Four Principles of Instruction

Wesley believed that parents should instruct their children *early, plainly, frequently,* and *patiently.* Let's see how each of these principles, informed by faith development theory (chap. 2), might help us as the primary teachers of our children.

Early Instruction

There is one obvious thing that Wesley's principle of early instruction tells us. *Christian nurture begins the moment a child arrives in this world!* There is also one obvious thing that Wesley's principle of early instruction does not mean. It does not mean the transference of "ideas" from our minds to the minds of our young children. We must remember that not until preadolescence (11 or 12 years old) do children begin to think in terms of concepts and ideas alone. Before this time, children must experience something in order to reason about it.

The principle of early instruction should cause us to think in terms of two things: caretaking and experience. Let us look at both of them.

Caretaking

Let's recap some of the things we learned in chapter 2 about faith development. We learned that faith begins in infancy, and it begins as a sense of trust. This sense of trust is communicated to the infant through the quality and consistency of care provided by parents or parentlike adults. The child senses whether this strange new world is safe and dependable or not. This sense of trust underlies all that comes later in faith development. On the other hand, if the needs of the infant are consistently delayed, or if the quality of care is consistently poor, the child does not learn to trust. This sense of mistrust tends to undermine faith development just as a sense of trust underlies it.

So how early does Christian nurture begin? Why, as soon as children go to school—first grade—of course. Wrong! It begins the moment a child arrives in this world. And how should parents carry out this early teaching of their children? Why, through explanations, of course. Wrong again! Parents begin to teach by lovingly and consistently caring for their children.

Wesley's principle of early instruction should cause us to think in terms of not only caretaking but experience.

Experience

Caretaking is a form of experience, but experience (as the term is used here) means much more than caretaking. Quite simply, the role of the parent is not to provide young children explanations but to encourage their curiosity and activity. We learned in chapter 2 that preschool- and early elementary-age children typically act with "experienced" faith. This says that the most important and fundamental form of learning is experience. We get so caught up in the habit of telling people things—especially our children—that we forget the tremendous value of experience. Krista and Brandon visiting a sheep barn (chap. 2) and that evening talking about Jesus, our Good Shepherd, brought the concept of experienced faith close to home.

We'll talk more about the importance of experience to a child's faith later. Let's just remember that Wesley's principle of early instruction consists of two things: the way we interact with our children (caretaking), and the way our children interact with us and their world (experience).

Plain Instruction

When Wesley exhorted parents and others to use words that the little children understand, building thoughts on the small concepts held by the little ones,[2] he was giving excellent advice. Let us seek to understand why this is so.

There are a couple of words that describe the reasoning process. They are the words *assimilate* and *accommodate.* Children (as well as adults) assimilate or interpret each new experience in terms of what they have already experienced or what they already know. When they cannot do this, they accommodate or change their understanding to fit the experience. For example, let's say three-year-old Jonathan falls and seriously cuts his forehead. He is rushed to the hospital in an ambulance. Afterward, when talking about the experience with his parents, he says he was taken to the hospital in a fire truck. Telling Jonathan that he meant ambulance instead of fire truck does not help. Jonathan was assimilating a new experience—ambulances—with something that he already knew—fire trucks. In order for him to make the change from fire truck to ambulance, he would have to accommodate or develop a new understanding—one that included ambulances, hospitals, doctors, and nurses.[3]

Wesley's advice to "graft" our teachings to what children already know is a good example of assimilation. It suggests, for example, that the Bible becomes meaningful for children when adults learn how to "tap" the understandings children already bring to the learning process. To say it another way, the Bible must be connected (grafted) to familiar areas of children's lives if they are going to understand it at all. This does not mean that we should never introduce them to anything new. It means that we should start with what children already know and expand outward from that.

Frequent Instruction

Question: "How often do you feed your children physically?" Answer: "Three meals a day, usually." Question: "How often do you feed your children spiritually?" Answer: *"(long pause)* Ahhhh, once a week on Sunday—most of the time." Do you know what Wesley would say to that? Do you know what Wesley *did* say to that? "Is the soul of less value than the body?"[4]

May I be blunt? Once a week on Sundays is simply far too little! Even the child who never misses Sunday School and children's church is only going to be exposed to a little more than 100 hours of teaching a year! Do we realize how short a time span is involved for the average child to watch 100 hours of television? The truth is, if we're really concerned about bringing up our children in the Christian faith, we're going to have to take seriously Wesley's principle of frequent instruction. This chapter includes some ideas on this vital area, but here are a couple of suggestions. First, establish a daily or regular time for the family to be together for devotional purposes. This might be at bedtime with younger children, or around the dinner table with preadolescents and teenagers. Second, continue your teaching throughout the day with younger children. Repeat the story, mention the prayer requests again, and sing the songs you are using in your times together. This will serve to reinforce your efforts with them.[5]

A word of caution needs to be inserted about Wesley's principle of frequent or repeated instruction, though. Older children think more logically and efficiently than do younger children, not just because they have more information, but because they are able to process that information differently. They possess some mental capabilities that their younger counterparts simply do not have.[6] This means that the effectiveness of frequent or repeated instruction in young children is limited. It will always be possible to make young children store up things in their memories and repeat them on request, but this does not necessarily imply understanding. Remember, they think differently than do older children and adults. Parents of young children should work at relating whatever is to be learned to the familiar areas of a child's life instead of expecting a playback of facts at the end of each Bible story.

On the other hand, we should not minimize the importance of memorization or rote learning either. Have you ever noticed how incredibly fast young children pick up things without any effort at learning them? This was driven home to me when I began praying the Lord's Prayer at bedtime for our children to recite. It wasn't too long before they were getting ahead of me, particularly Krista. So I asked her one evening to pray the Lord's Prayer without any help. She did not miss one single word. There were not even any long pauses. She had learned it by heart, listening to her dad repeat it night after night. The same obviously holds true for the learning of Scripture verses as well. Even though their understanding is limited (one night she asked what "debtors" meant), repetition during the early years will imprint a rich treasury of spiritual truths and facts in their minds; that storehouse can be drawn on at will for the rest of their lives. This is particularly true for older children and early adolescents (8 to 9 years old to 14 to 15 years old). During these years, children are able to memorize and retain huge amounts of detail, with an efficiency apparently superior to any other period of life.[7] The spiritual significance of this should be obvious.

Patient Instruction

In the day of the "hurried child," Wesley's principle of patient instruction would be well to remember. In her book *Developing Spiritually Sensitive Children,* Olive J. Alexander tells about an incident involving her five- and seven-year-olds. The two children had baked cookies by themselves—without permission, of course—and were now distributing the treats among guests Mrs. Alexander was entertaining. Surprisingly, the cookies were delicious. One of the guests even asked the children for the recipe. When it got to the part that dealt with oven temperature, one of them said, "Well, I didn't turn it on high. Only to 200 degrees." Mrs. Alexander figured that the "long, slow bake in the oven at half the usual cookie-baking temperature" explained part of the cookies' deliciousness. It got her to thinking.

> Children's growth is likewise slow. . . . [God's] Spirit is actively involved in their developmental processes—processes which cannot be rushed. We need to follow God's clock and not devise our own timetables. . . . In the same way that each cooking recipe is arranged in steps which are often dependent upon each other, so a child's social, physical, and spiritual development is arranged in successive steps. As a result, they can move smoothly and successively through their current developmental stage only when they have successfully grown through the preceding stages.[8]

Did you catch that? Children are like slow-baked cookies whose developmental capabilities should not be rushed. This means that we, as parents, must be patient with our children and persevering in our teachings with them.

But what about the child who does not seem to respond? What about the young person who seemingly has turned his back on Mom and Dad's religion? Obviously, there is no guarantee that the efforts of the most diligent parent will ever be rewarded. Our children are free moral agents and must choose for themselves. On the other hand, Wesley encouraged us not to get discouraged and to not ever, ever, ever give up praying for our children. "Possibly the 'bread' which you have 'cast upon the waters' may be 'found after many days.' The seed which has long remained in the ground may, at length, spring up into a plentiful harvest. Especially if you do not restrain prayer before God, if you continue instant herein with all supplications."[9]

Wesley has touched upon one of the most important factors in the Christian faith development of our children: *prayer!* It is advice that we parents need to hear, particularly parents of teenagers in the stage of searching faith. Yet surely we should pray over every stage of our children's faith development and spiritual training. It is the most important part to Wesley's principle of patient instruction. We are called to act as priests, or bridge builders, to our children. In liturgical worship, a priest sometimes faces the congregation and sometimes faces the altar. These two stances are significant. They symbolize the two basic functions of a priest. When he faces the congregation, he represents God to the people. When he faces the altar, he represents the people to God. Similarly, the "priesthood of parents" involves two basic things. First, parents represent God to their children. They do this in a variety of ways, which we will discuss in the remainder of this chapter and the next. Second, parents represent their children to God. They do this primarily through intercessory prayer![10]

I think one of the most dramatic examples of this—presenting our children to God through intercessory prayer—is told by psychologist James Dobson. He tells how his great-grandfather, in the final decades of his life, spent the hour from eleven to twelve o'clock every day in intercessory prayer for his children and generations of children not yet born. Before he died, the old man felt that God had given him an unusual promise: that the next four generations of his family would all be Christians. To make a positively thrilling story brief, James Dobson represents the fourth generation, *all* of whom have been Christians! Dobson records, "It staggers the mind to realize that the prayers of this one man, spoken more than fifty years ago, reach across four generations of time and influence developments in my life today. That is the power of prayer and the source of my hope and optimism."[11]

Parents, pray without ceasing for your children! Set aside regular times to pray and fast only for them. There is too much against them, and the stakes are way too high for us to give any less. Pray! *Pray!* PRAY!

Now that we've looked at Wesley's four principles of instruction, let's move on to what I call his three essentials of instruction. To assist parents, preachers, and schoolmasters in the religious instruction of the young, Wesley prepared several textbooks and tracts. A study of these resources suggests three essentials of religious instruction: Scripture, prayer, and music.

Wesley's Three Essentials of Instruction

Scripture

The idea of faith development tells us that the age of a child determines the approach to teaching! This is particularly true when it comes to teaching children the Bible. The important thing to remember is this: The Bible must be connected or tied (Wesley said "grafted") to familiar areas of a child's life if he is to understand it at all. Now let's turn our attention to some of the ways we can assist our children in the development of Bible learning.

We can think in terms of four kinds of Bible knowledge: the content or facts of the Bible, the meaning of the Bible, the background of the Bible, and the skills involved in the use of the Bible. The development of this knowledge begins in childhood and expands in youth. Of these four kinds of knowledge, facts and meanings are the most important Bible-learning tasks of childhood. This learning of facts and meanings takes place in a special way. Children "experience" the facts of the Bible and "discover" the meanings of the Bible.

Experiencing Bible Content

Since Bible stories will account for much of the biblical materials used with children, the ability of parents to tell stories is important. This does not mean that Bible stories should be read only. Stories can and should be told, sung, dramatized, and expressed through a variety of visual aids and activities. Visual aids such as puppets, flannelgraphs, blocks, and art—to name just a few—can help children learn biblical facts. Other activities can do the same. For example, children can search their room for a well-hidden dime and then hear the story of the lost coin (Luke 15:8-10). They can reenact, with toy boats in their own bathtub, the story of Jesus and His disciples caught by the storm (Mark 4:35-41). They can paint a picture of how it feels to be lost and found, then hear the story of the lost sheep (Luke 15:1-7). They can be led through an experience of what it feels like to be hot, tired, and thirsty in the desert, then hear the story of the Exodus. They can observe baptism in the sanctuary, then hear the story of Jesus' baptism (Matt. 3:13-17).[12]

If our children have asked this question once, they have asked it 100 times: "Daddy, are we going to do our 'play' tonight?" "Play" refers to an informal but guided dramatization of a Bible story that involves our whole family.[13] In our plays the whole family dresses up in bathrobes and bath-towel turbans (you ought to see us) before we read the story. Afterward we assign parts and act it out in an informal but guided dramatization. "Guided" means that Daddy or Mommy ends up being "director." Guided dramatization differs from role playing—where people practice putting themselves in the situation of others—in that there is little structure in true role playing. This lack of structure, along with their limited ability to take someone else's point of view, makes role playing difficult to use with children under the age of 9 or 10. Informal but guided dramatization of Bible stories is more suitable for younger children.[14] Brandon's favorite play is the story of the Good Samaritan. He always wants to be the robber so he can beat up his Samaritan sister. Some of our plays are downright hysterical but always fun and meaningful. Through these and other activities, our children are "experiencing Bible content."

Discovering and Expressing Bible Meanings

After children have experienced Bible content, there are four levels at which they begin to discover meanings. The first level is, *What does it mean to* me *right now—as a child?* Parents can facilitate this discovery in several ways. One way is by listening to children and hearing meanings when they are spontaneously expressed. Have you ever noticed how theological children's statements tend to be sometimes? "Why can't I see God?" "Where is heaven?" "But I don't want Grandma to be in heaven. I want her to be here with me." Then there's the lighter side. "Daddy, what keeps people in heaven from falling through the clouds?" (Wings, of course!) And then there's the time I asked Krista how Moses got up the mountain to get the Ten Commandments. She answered, "Ski lift!" The point is this: We learn about the understandings children have about the Bible by listening to them. Listening and talking is an important way we share our faith with our children.

Another way parents can facilitate the discovery of Bible meanings is by asking questions and encouraging responses. "Why do you think that?" "Whom did you like best in the story?" "Why?" "What would you have done?" Responses do not always have to be verbal, either. Parents can suggest that the child draw, color, or paint a picture about the story or how the story made the child feel. Children can also act out the story through puppets, guided dramatization, or role play. Such activities often reveal how the child has heard and interpreted the biblical material.[15]

Wesley's method of instruction consisted largely of asking questions and hearing responses. We said earlier that he was more concerned with a child's understanding of the Bible than retention of Bible facts. "Beware of . . . making children parrots, instead of Christians," said Wesley. "Labour that . . . they may understand every single sentence which they read. . . . Turn each sentence every way, propose it in every light, and question them continually on every point."[16] Asking questions and encouraging both verbal and nonverbal responses is an important way we can help our children discover Bible meanings.

The second level at which children begin to discover Bible meanings is, *What does it mean to you—my parent?* At this level, parents share their own responses with the child. The point is not necessarily to correct a wrong idea or give a dogmatic answer, but to share ourselves and our faith with them. Responses to the child's statements may take varied forms. "I think that, too." "That's a new idea!" "I've never thought about it like that before." "To me it means . . ." "I used to think that, too. Now I think . . ." As a result, children learn that the most important people in their lives share something important with them.

The third level of Bible meaning is, *What did it mean to them—the people of the Bible?* With older elementary and some early elementary children, parents can ask, "What do you think this story meant to the very first people who heard it?" This helps children realize that the Bible stories are not mere happenings in history. It says to them that the Bible and its stories had meaning for people long ago, too.

The fourth level of Bible meaning is, *What does it mean to us—the Church today?* Older elementary children can begin to think what a particular Bible story or passage might mean if taken seriously by the whole Church today. Once again, parent and child share with each other. At this point, the child's personal understanding of the Bible has expanded to include the meanings it has for other Christians, past and present. A movement through these four levels of Bible meaning during childhood prepares the way for a possible fifth level of meaning in adolescence: *What has the Bible meant to us—the Church historically?*

A brief word about Bible skills should be added here. By the time most children finish their elementary years, they should be able to find Bible references. This may include the use of a simple concordance and a child's Bible dictionary, and perhaps even the awareness that there are such things as commentaries. Parents can not only let their children see them using such tools, but a casual suggestion to "look it up" will often send children to the Bible. Parents can also use games to teach skills; in "sword drills" children are rewarded for quickly finding references in their Bibles. Such training, however, should probably be used on an individual basis and not as competition between children. Competition easily becomes a win/lose exercise in which the same children generally lose. How fast a reference is found is not nearly as important as that it is found.[17]

Prayer

Prayer was another essential in John Wesley's method of formal instruction. He believed education in prayer to be a vital part of the religious upbringing of children. Children should be taught not only to pray but also how to pray.

It is helpful, for parents desiring to educate their children in prayer, to know the understandings children have about prayer. Up to 7 years, children pray easily, usually about the practical happenings in their lives, but with very little understanding of its meaning. From 7 to 9 years, children express prayer as an appropriate activity that tends to be rather routine and ritualized—prior to eating, before going to bed, at church, and so on. Seven- to 9-year-olds still do not typically rise above the outward behaviors associated with prayer to its meaning. At age 9 or 10, and increasingly thereafter, prayer begins to emerge as conversation with God. At this point, prayer becomes much more personal and individualized than routinized and scheduled. Preadolescents tend to pray anytime about their needs and feelings and not just at bedtime or before meals. Prayer begins to take on adult meanings.[18]

These three stages of prayer imply several things for parents. Since young children pray typically about the practical happenings in their lives, parents should make it a point to pray in the child's world. Everything from Krista's dolls and the dog to Brandon's cut finger and the neighbor's cat gets prayed for around our house. Sometimes this becomes quite taxing before meals, especially when Mom and Dad are hungry. Usually there has to be a little intervention (not divine) by my wife or me saying, "And thank You, God, for our food—Amen." The point is, we should pray in the child's world, not our adult world.

Since the prayers of younger children also tend to be somewhat routine and ritualized, there should be regular times of prayer. Our family observes the ritual of always holding hands and praying before mealtimes at home. A different family member usually prays before each meal. In addition, the children rarely go to sleep without a bedtime prayer. It is so much a part of their lives that they usually cannot go to sleep without it. Sometimes the kids are tired, and their prayers reflect it. At other times their bedtime prayers are expressed with much feeling. Just like any adult, a child's ability and desire to pray will vary, and that should be respected by the parent.

During these regular times of prayer—particularly at bedtime—parents have the wonderful opportunity to teach children the various aspects or forms of prayer; like adoration (praise), confession, thanksgiving, intercession, and petition for oneself.[19] This can be accomplished by the child hearing the parent pray these prayers and/or the parent guiding the child in praying these prayers. For example, the child could be asked to thank God for the beautiful day (thanksgiving) or pray for Uncle Jim's upcoming operation (intercession). For variety in our prayers for others, we have even selected certain people to pray for on particular days of the week. On Monday night, we pray for our family, near and far; on Tuesday night, our church family; on Wednesday night, our school friends; and so on. Occasionally, at the close of our own prayers or in the place of our own prayers, the kids want to recite the Lord's Prayer after Dad or Mom. Our bedtime prayers are always kept brief.

Obviously, children will be encouraged to pray if they see and hear their parents pray. Author Olive J. Alexander tells how her small children would often climb out of bed in the mornings and find her praying on the sofa. She said, "This was the beginning of a heritage of daily prayer and praise. It wasn't necessary for me to tell them they should pray. . . . Instead they observed my conduct."[20]

I have similarly tried to beat the family out of bed in the mornings to have a quiet cup of coffee. This quiet time usually includes devotional reading and prayer. Occasionally, one or both of the kids will stray out of bed and catch me praying. This is precisely what I want them to do! I want them to catch their dad praying; hopefully that image will stay with them throughout their lives.

Music

Though less dominant, perhaps, than Scripture and prayer, John Wesley used music as a third essential for teaching children. Singing together does offer parents a fine opportunity for teaching children. Regular devotional times can be used to teach songs and sing together, or more spontaneous times—like in the car, on vacations, while working—can be used. Musical ability, or the lack thereof, does not have to affect anyone's enjoyment or participation in the least. With younger children, short, simple songs or choruses (with repetitious phrases if possible), action songs, rhythm instruments, and taped or recorded music are just some of the resources parents can use.[21] Our family tries to use one evening per week strictly for this purpose. With my guitar and the kids' rhythm instruments as accompaniment, we sing the choruses we have learned at church. It's especially enjoyable for Brandon, who knows he can bang his tambourine as loudly as he wishes without consequence. Not only is this time spent singing fun, it's educational.

The remainder of this chapter is geared to helping us think seriously about this matter of family worship today.

Family Worship

"Do you believe that regular and meaningful family worship is possible today?" I asked that question to a group of parents in my church, and 80 percent of them responded, "No!" Their reasons varied. A few of them shared bad memories of Mom and Dad dragging them into the back bedroom every night for an hour or so of family devotions. Ugh! Most of them, however, gave busy schedules and lack of meaning as the major reasons. What about you? Do you believe it is possible today?

A study was conducted several years ago of church families in one denomination. It was found that 7 of 10 families had grace at meals, but only 1 in 20 had Scripture reading in family groups. The researchers concluded that if this is even approximately representative, then the traditional model of family devotions does not meet the needs of Christian families today. It has been said that for many church people today, family worship is "a romanticized vision of father and mother gathering their children around them for hymns, scripture reading and prayer."[22]

Perhaps your experience is different. Family worship or family devotions in your home are working and meaningful. If so, the old saying "If it ain't broke, don't fix it" is for you. On the other hand, maybe family worship in your home definitely needs "fixin'." If so, let's not hoist up the white flag of surrender just yet. Let's consider two different but complementary approaches to family worship today: family worship as "special rituals," and family worship as "regular celebrations."

Family Worship as Special Rituals

There's no doubt about it. You're busy, I'm busy, all God's children are busy; but (you're not going to like me for this) busy schedules and lack of time are *not* our problem. We have enough time to do what we feel is important! Instead, what is lacking is "the will and the imagination to express symbolically the deeper meanings of family events in an appropriate way."[23] What that means is that families can use special occasions—like birthdays and holidays—for the development of religious rituals in the home. Family rituals or traditions are a powerful way we can share our faith with our children.

Family worship as special rituals or traditions can be structured around two things: *special occasions,* like birthdays, weddings, and vacations; and *holidays or seasons of the year,* like Thanksgiving, Christmas, and Easter. There are many examples I could give, but there is one New Year's Eve ritual I really like, particularly with older children. On New Year's Eve the family gathers around the fireplace with popcorn, drinks, and a calendar of the year just passed. The evening is spent tearing off the sheets of each month, starting with January. Each member takes turns trying to remember what he did, felt, or experienced that month. A special effort is made to share how God was real during the high or low times that month. After each month, into the fire goes the page, symbolizing that the old year is gone. Right through the year you go, sharing, listening, laughing, and crying. The evening is concluded with a prayer of thanks to God for allowing you to be a family and for being with you the whole year long.[24]

Isn't that beautiful and meaningful? Some family traditions will be less elaborate than this one, while others will be more elaborate. But do you see how special occasions can be used for the development of religious traditions in the home? Think how the rituals in your church—say, baptism or Communion—provide you with a special sense of God's presence and love. Family rituals are no different! They provide a special sense of God's presence between Sundays. What it takes, parents, is the will and the imagination to express symbolically the deeper meanings of family events in an appropriate way. I would encourage you to make a list of those things that you're probably already doing as a family. My wife and I did this separately and then compared notes. One of the things we discovered is that trimming the Christmas tree around our house is a *big* deal. The evening begins with a "Happy Birthday, Jesus!" party. After dinner, my wife serves the cake she has baked with the letters "Happy Birthday, Jesus" on it. The kids light the candles, and we all sing happy birthday to Jesus. After we finish eating the cake, we turn on Christmas music and begin the long but enjoyable process of trimming the tree. This has become an annual ritual around our house, and the kids start talking about it weeks in advance. Together we celebrate the true meaning of Christmas—the birth of our Lord and Savior Jesus Christ!

Family Worship as Regular Celebrations

Family worship as special rituals is *not* to suggest that families should neglect Scripture, prayer, and even music on a more regular basis. It is the regular times of family worship that hold the greatest potential for heightening God-consciousness in the family. By the way, *regular* does not necessarily mean daily or even every other day. It might mean once a week—say, a family night. Notice too I use the word *celebrations* instead of *devotions*. *Devotions* carries the idea of private prayer, while *celebrations* implies togetherness and enjoyment.[25]

I said earlier in this chapter that parents should think in terms of a daily or regular time for the family to be together for worship. This might mean at bedtime with children or around the dinner table with preadolescents and teenagers. Let's think first about regular celebrations with stage one and stage two children.

Stage One Children (2 or 3 years old to 6 or 7 years old) and Stage Two Children (6 or 7 years old to 11 or 12 years old)

Look back at the section in this chapter headed "Wesley's Three Essentials of Instruction." Everything talked about there applies to regular celebrations with children. The important thing to remember is that celebrations *must* be attractive and enjoyable. Visual aids, such as puppets, flannelgraphs, blocks, and artwork as well as dramatization of Bible stories are ways to make regular celebrations both interesting and educational. Remember to keep them short and informal —brief celebrations, usually five minutes or so, will do. Make them even shorter when children are particularly tired. Dramatizations will usually take longer, but most children won't mind. They will probably not want to stop. Besides, you probably won't be using dramatizations every time, either.

Whatever methods and materials are used with children, emphasis should probably be on Bible stories, since the hearing, telling, and retelling of stories is an important characteristic of children's faith—especially stage two faith. Because stage two children in particular tend to be somewhat structured and orderly, they will probably expect celebrations to be conducted on a regular basis. While stage two children grasp more than stage one children, they usually have not developed the indifference that some teenagers show. This suggests that childhood—especially the elementary-age years—is a prime period for family worship as regular celebrations.

Preadolescents and Stage Three Adolescents

Toward the end of stage two (11 or 12 years old, if not earlier), parents will probably find that worship times and methods need changing. Gone are the days of puppets and flannelgraphs. Teenagers should probably be required to meet with the family for worship whenever possible, but their participation should not be forced. Celebrations should be kept brief.[26]

For many families with preadolescents and teenagers, dinnertime is often the best group time for family worship. In fact, family expert Delores Curran believes that families with teenagers will usually find the period immediately following dinner the best time. She feels that it is hard to get the family together at any other part of the day.[27] I hear some of you saying, "But we can't even get the whole family together for dinner!" Consider this. Virginia Satir reminds us that families go through a splitting-up process each day—they leave each other in the morning. She says that it is wise for families also to go through a reconciliation process at least once a day—to come back together again in the evening—and touch base with each other. In the busy lives that most of us lead, such a meeting cannot be left to chance—it has to be planned. She recommends dinnertime as the best time for many families. Families that work different hours must simply invent new times to come together for family planning and business.

If you're a family that's having difficulty finding a time for everyone to get together, here's a suggestion. Take a sheet of paper for each family member and divide it up according to the hours in a day. Start when the first person gets out of bed and continue until the hour that the last person goes to bed. For example, if the first person gets up at 5:30 A.M. and the last person goes to bed at 12:00 midnight, your sheets would look like this:

5:30 A.M.	12:30 P.M.	7:30 P.M.
6:30 A.M.	1:30 P.M.	8:30 P.M.
7:30 A.M.	2:30 P.M.	9:30 P.M.
8:30 A.M.	3:30 P.M.	10:30 P.M.
9:30 A.M.	4:30 P.M.	11:30 P.M.
10:30 A.M.	5:30 P.M.	12:00 P.M.
11:30 A.M.	6:30 P.M.	

All members keep records of where they are every hour for *two days* out of a week—one weekday and one weekend day. At the end of the two-day period, one person puts the records all together and tabulates the results. This will dramatically and often surprisingly show the times available to each family member to be alone (self time), to each family member to be with one other family member (pair time), and to all family members to be together (group time).[28] It's the group time in which you're primarily interested for family worship.

If dinnertime is usually the best time for many families to touch base every day, then that may also be the best time for family worship. I remember, as a college student, worshiping with a family that had three teenagers. It was the practice of that family to use five minutes or so immediately following dinner for worship. The father read a short scripture, prayed briefly, then led the rest of the family in the recitation of the Lord's Prayer. That was it! That was their regular practice—short and simple, meaningful and memorable. The kids still talk about that time to this day.

Variations to this example are many. Depending on the family, parents might occasionally consider using scripture that relates to the issues adolescents face. For example, regarding the issue of peer pressure, family members might discuss the crowd who called for Jesus' crucifixion. Regarding sexual morality, the incident between Joseph and Potiphar's wife might be discussed. Other issues might include dating, money, attitudes toward education, and leaving home.

Here's an interesting approach that can be used with Bible narratives. Let's take the story of the paralytic who was let down through the roof for Jesus to heal in Mark 2:1-12. Discuss it at two levels. First, on the objective level, one asks, "What do you feel is the central meaning of this passage?" and "How does it apply to our lives?" Each family member is given the opportunity to share, but sharing is strictly optional. Second, on the subjective level, family members are instructed to put themselves in the place of each character in the story through private reflection. The first question might be, "Now let yourself be the paralytic. What emotional or spiritual part of you is in need of help from others? In what sense do you feel paralyzed, unable to do what you want to do by your own willpower?" Allow time for reflection. Then move to the next character and ask, "Now be one of the four men who brought the paralytic to Jesus. What aspect of your personality wants to help that 'paralyzed' part of yourself, or maybe help someone else?" Again, allow time for reflection. Move on to the Jewish scribes in the story and ask, "What part of you is like the scribes, harshly judging and being more concerned with correct ways of thinking and doing than getting healed and being free?" Finally, family members can be asked to be like Jesus and to experience that part of oneself that is forgiving and loving. After this time of private reflection, someone may want to share his feelings, but let it be strictly on a volunteer basis.[29]

Just as the Wesleyan essential of Scripture can be used in a nontraditional way, so can the Wesleyan essential of prayer. Instead of the same person always praying, different family members can take turns praying, or maybe all family members can pray conversationally. In conversational praying, one person picks up where the last person left off and prays sentence prayers. Another suggestion is for one person to lead the rest of the family in guided prayers. One person shares a request for the rest of the family to pray for silently. This is also an excellent way for parents to teach children the different moods of prayer—adoration or praise, confession, thanksgiving, intercession, petition, and meditation. For example, "Uncle Jim is scheduled to enter the hospital tomorrow for surgery. Let's pray for him right now." A few moments are given for silent intercessory prayer, then the family is instructed to pray a silent prayer of thanksgiving. "Now let's thank Him for hearing us and promising to meet all our needs." A final suggestion—to be used with care—is for all family members to pray aloud at the same time. This does not mean distractingly loud, but loudly enough to be heard.[30] It's not something you will probably want to use all the time, but think how often many of us pray out loud together at church.

There is one final problem. It is the problem of faith

stage differences. What do you do when you have, for example, 2 stage three adolescents and 1 stage one preschooler in the family? Obviously, children are not all at the same age or the same stage. Do you gear your celebrations toward the older or younger members of the family? There may not be a perfect answer to that question, but consider trying this: Aim the center of interest toward the older children in the family. Younger children will usually grasp something, but older children will quickly lose interest if the material or method is too elementary. You might consider giving younger children something to do or look at during the worship time and maybe have a separate time for them later—say, before bedtime.[31] This may not be the best solution, but it is one possibility.

Obviously, parents are not the only source of spiritual training in a child's life, but they are the primary source. Hopefully, some of the principles and essentials discussed in this chapter have been helpful. There is one final dimension to John Wesley's method of religious instruction. Wesley understood instruction to be both formal *and informal.* In fact, this matter of informal instruction might mean more to our children's Christian faith than anything else we've talked about so far. Let's turn to it now in the final chapter.

DISCUSSION QUESTIONS

1. Discuss the statement: "We need to live as though we are the only available source of spiritual training for our children."

2. How important is intercessory prayer to Christian child rearing?

105

3. What are some ways parents can teach their children in and through:

    a. Scripture?

    b. prayer?

    c. music?

4. Do you believe that regular and meaningful family worship is possible today? Why or why not?

5. Make a list and/or discuss some of your present family traditions and rituals.

6. Family therapist Virginia Satir says it is wise for families to come together at least once every day. What time of the day does your family usually come together? Is that a good time for family worship? Why or why not?

6

Catch the Faith

(Informal Instruction)

Do you feel qualified to teach your child religion? Some may be thinking in reply, Me? Qualified to teach my child religion? Are you serious?

I remember asking that question, "Do you feel qualified to teach your child religion?" to a group of Christian parents. One father gave a straightforward, matter-of-fact answer: "Yes, I feel very qualified to teach my child religion." You could gauge how surprising his answer was by the stares he received from the rest of the group. I had to bite my lip to keep from laughing at their reactions.

Unlike that very candid and confident father, there are many, many Christian parents who do not feel qualified to teach their children religion. If you are one of them, here is another little exercise for you. Take a few minutes to write down every conceivable reason why you feel unqualified to teach your child religion. Don't read any farther until you have written down your answers or have at least given it serious thought. Do that right now.

Have you finished? Now go back through your list and apply those very same reasons to your teaching of sanitation, manners, compassion, fairness, and any of the other lessons of life we parents teach our children. Your reasoning doesn't hold up, does it? The point is this: We don't hesitate teaching our children certain subjects just because we've never been formally trained in those subjects. For example, we don't hesitate teaching our children sanitation just because we've never had a course in health education. We don't hesitate teaching our children manners just because we've never had a course in etiquette. We don't hesitate teaching our children fairness just because we've never had a course in ethics. We are successful teachers in many subjects, possibly because we do not realize we are teaching. So why do we hesitate teaching our children religion? *Why?* Because many of us have grown up believing that religion must be formally taught by people who have been formally trained to do so.[1] Fellow parents, nothing could be further from the truth!

John Wesley believed that parents should instruct their children formally, but he also believed that parents should instruct their children informally. He believed that parents should not only teach their children through the somewhat formal use of Scripture, prayer, and music, but also through the informal use of life experiences—the unexpected and unplanned happenings of each day. This is the kind of thing we are going to talk about in this final chapter. We're also going to look at two additional ways we teach our children informally. One is by marital harmony, and the other is by personal example. Let's begin now by looking at this matter of informal teaching through life experiences.

Informal Teaching Through Life Experiences

There's no question that Christian parents should use the Bible to teach their children. John Wesley saw Scripture as one of the major essentials of religious instruction. The question is, must parents always use the Bible with children to be described as "teaching biblically"? What's your opinion? We have already said that when the Bible is used with children, it must be taught experientially. That is, the Bible must be related to familiar areas of a child's life if he is to understand it at all. But must a parent *always* use the Bible with children to be described as "teaching biblically"? The answer is no. Parents can and should use the everyday experiences of life to teach children, if those experiences are related back to the Bible.[2] Let us make this point clearer.

In chapters 3 and 5 we learned about Wesley's four principles of religious instruction: that it should be early, plain, frequent, and patient. In his discussion of that second principle—plain instruction—Wesley used a very informal experience to teach a child something about God. He pictured a parent and child walking together outdoors. The parent looks up and uses the sun to illustrate God and His love.[3]

Wesley further advised parents to pray that God would use such informal experiences to teach children.

> While you are speaking in this, or some such manner, you should be continually lifting up your heart to God, beseeching him to open the eyes of their understanding, and to pour his light upon them. He, and he alone, can make them to differ herein from the beasts that perish. He alone can apply your words to their hearts; without which all your labour will be in vain. But whenever the Holy Ghost teaches, there is no delay in learning.[4]

This one, brief reference is enough to know that John Wesley did not limit teaching to formal instruction. He urged parents to use the unplanned happenings of each day. The first time I read this illustration of Wesley's, I thought about Deut. 6:7, where parents are instructed to use the informal settings of life to teach children. It reads, "Impress [these commandments] on your children. Talk about them when you sit at home and when you walk along the road, when you lie down and when you get up" (NIV). Think about that! We parents transmit our religious convictions in the ways we talk with our children, walk with them, put them to bed at night, and greet them in the morning. That covers just about the whole day and everything in between, doesn't it? The problem with many of us, including myself, is that we're usually not thinking in those terms. We think that we should share our Christian faith only in the formal and planned times—at church and in our family worship. Deut. 6:7 and John Wesley are telling us to share our faith *all day long!* Share it in the informal settings and the unplanned happenings of each day. Until we begin to see this, there will always be an important dimension missing to the faith sharing in our home.

Let's look at another example of teaching children through unplanned happenings. Let's say our three-year-old drops his gum on the floor at the grocery store. What do we do? We stop our shopping, throw away the gum, and explain that the floor is dirty. We tell him that the floor has germs and that he might get sick from chewing it. The child asks, "What are germs?" and we translate our knowledge of microbiology into his three-year-old understanding. We do it and don't give it a second thought. Teaching good health habits is one of our responsibilities as parents, and we accept it. But what happens when our three-year-old wanders up to the checkout counter and opens up a package of gum without our paying for it? Suddenly it's not just sanitation that we're teaching, but religion. Do we explain to the child that the gum isn't ours and must be paid for? When the child asks, "Why can't I take it? There are lots there for everyone," do we take the time to translate our knowledge of morality and personal property to the child? Or do we spank him and tell him it's naughty?[5]

I shared this with a group of parents in my church, and one young father told about an incident involving his elementary-age son. One afternoon, the boy arrived home from school with a *Playboy* magazine tucked under his arm. Trying hard to appear calm, the father cleared his throat and asked where he got it. The son explained that he found it in the school yard. Rather than grab the magazine and issue a stern warning to never look at anything like that again, the two of them sat down and talked about it. Obviously the boy had several questions, and the father used that opportunity to share his Christian convictions about the human body and morality. Now didn't that father deserve an A+ for informally teaching his son through a *very* unplanned experience? How do you think you might have reacted under similar circumstances?

Can you see what the Scriptures and Wesley want us to do? They are telling us to use some of the informal, unexpected, and unplanned happenings of each day to teach our Christian faith, for we already use them to teach so many other lessons of life. This does not mean that we should go around attaching a spiritual lesson to *every* experience! I can't think of anything that will turn children off faster. What it does mean is that we should be on the lookout for appropriate opportunities to teach our children. Common sense ought to tell us how much or how little.

Let's turn our attention now from the teaching that comes through unplanned happenings to the teaching that comes from a good marriage.

Informal Teaching Through Marital Harmony

We've talked a lot about Wesley's sermon "On Family Religion." He used as his text Josh. 24:15: "As for me and my house, we will serve the Lord." Wesley asked three questions in that sermon: "What [does it mean] to 'serve the Lord'?" "Who are included in that expression, 'my house'?" and, "What can we do, that we and our house may serve the Lord?" Most of our attention has been focused on that third question: "What can we do . . . ?" It is here that Wesley discussed his twofold method of Christian child rearing—discipline and instruction. Let's look now at his discussion of the second question. Just who are included in that expression "my house"? Wesley said that a parent's first responsibility in the home was *not* to the children. Surprised?

Wesley understood the expression "my house" to mean *the wife first, then the children!* In other words, a father's first responsibility in the home was to the children's mother, and vice versa.

> The person in your house that claims your first and nearest attention, is, undoubtedly, your wife; seeing you are to love her, even as Christ hath loved the Church, when he laid down his life for it, that he might "purify it unto himself, not having spot, or wrinkle, or any such thing." The same end is every husband to pursue, in all his intercourse with his wife; to use every possible means that she may be freed from every spot, and may walk unblamable in love.
>
> Next to your wife are your children.[6]

Wesley reminds me of a counselor whom I once read about, who was asked a very probing question by one father. The father felt that he had failed as a parent and asked the counselor, "If your children were small again, what would you do?" The counselor's thoughts about that question developed into a book. Each chapter was devoted to something the counselor would do differently were he starting his family again. Guess what he said he would do first. He said he would love his wife more! That is, he would be freer to let his children know that he loved their mother. When children see expressions of love in the home and know that parents love each other, there is a security and stability that comes in no other way.[7]

If it is true that children experience security and stability as a result of marital harmony, then the opposite of that is also true. Whether it be daily screaming matches and outright violence or stony silences and bitter sarcasms, the one thing that most often throws children into emotional isolation is

112

conflict between parents. Blinded by the passion of an argument or by their own resentful feelings, parents do not realize how deeply their children are being torn apart inwardly because of their conflict. One young person said, "My first disillusionment goes back to when I realized that my parents did not get on together. It was terrible. I felt utterly alone and rebellious against life." Instinctively, children want and try to keep parents united, but they often feel utterly helpless to do so. It is this feeling of helplessness that crushes children.[8] Virginia Satir thinks that there is a direct relationship between marital harmony and successful child rearing (what she calls "peoplemaking").[9] I agree! The sooner that parents in conflict realize this—that the children are the real losers—the better!

For the remainder of this section, let's look briefly at some ways we can strengthen marriage during the child-rearing years.

Parents of Stage One Children
(2 or 3 years old to 6 or 7 years old)

In many, many ways, having a baby tests a marriage. That's nothing new, is it? One reason is that young couples have to adjust to becoming parents while they are still learning what it means to be a good husband or a good wife. The fatigue that results from caretaking (especially on the part of the mother), the lack of time to be alone together, the learning of new mothering and fathering skills, and the job responsibilities and pressures (particularly on the father) are just some of the reasons why marriages are tested at this stage.

One suggestion is for couples to share the responsibilities of parenting. Did you hear that, Dad? Share the load of parenting with your wife. This means giving her a break from the kids on a regular basis if she does not work outside the home. It means showing her love and respect and emotionally supporting her during this time. This is one suggestion where you need to do as I say and not as I do. If you don't understand that, my wife does!

Another suggestion is to work at your marriage, and one way to do this is by finding time to be alone together. *Many marriages jump the track by overinvesting in the children and underinvesting in the marriage!* This might mean going out regularly on a date, as you did before you got married.[10] I read about one husband who had what many would consider to be a peculiar habit. For years, he would take his wife out on a date every Thursday evening. He would come home from work early to shower, shave, and put on his best suit. He would then leave in the car for a few minutes, then return to ring his front doorbell. His wife would greet him at the door, and together they would sit and talk in the living room. After a while, they would go out to dinner or some other really nice place. When the evening was over, the man would escort his wife to the door and kiss her good-night. He would then drive his car into the garage and come in through the back door. Now it sounds silly for a man to do that with his wife, but is it any wonder that when that man died, his wife watered his grave with her tears?[11]

I shared this story in one of my sermons on the family, and the very next night one of my laymen showed up at his front door with a long-stemmed rose in his hand. When his wife opened the door, he presented her with the rose and asked her out for a date. He said she started laughing and did not stop laughing until after dinner. I'm not sure if they went out on that date or not.

Still another suggestion is to keep the communication lines open. Talk openly with each other about your marriage, the children, and your mutual interests outside the home. It's usually the hidden feelings of bitterness and resentment that sabotage a marriage.

A final suggestion is to acquaint yourself with some of the characteristics of normal child development. This will help you keep the otherwise perplexing aspects of child rearing from interfering with your marriage. Chapter 2 on faith development should be helpful at this point.

Parents of Stage Two Children
(6 or 7 years old to 11 or 12 years old)

The pressures on couples with stage two children are different from those of the previous period, but no less intense. In chapter 2, we saw how acquaintances and relationships outside the family circle begin to widen at stage two with the starting of school. This process gradually makes children less dependent on their parents emotionally. In turn, parents should gradually release children into their own orbits. This does not mean letting them go, but letting them grow up. Unfortunately there are many parents who have trouble doing this—particularly parents whose marriage is less than satisfying. When the marital relationship is not what it should be, it is easy for parents to make their children a substitute spouse. They begin to invest themselves emotionally into their children instead of each other. The problem is that God has designed the husband-wife relationship to gradually deepen over the years, while He has designed the parent-child relationship to gradually diminish. Parents cannot and should not expect the same degree of emotional intimacy with their children as they do with each other. It's not fair to anyone, especially the children.

Life with one or more elementary-age children is usually brimming with activities. The temptation for many couples is to become *so absorbed* in the flurry of activities—school, work, and church—*that the marriage relationship is more or less neglected!* Suggestions for couples at this stage are essentially the same as before, with one or two additions. During the school years, the identity of the family as a unit is as strong as it ever will be. Even though relationships are widening, children are still deeply involved in their own families. Parents should plan things together as a family, such as outings, picnics, trips, and vacations. In addition, parents should work at gradually releasing their children, while working to strengthen the marriage.

Parents of Stage Three Adolescents

The pressures of this period are many and varied. Conflicts between parents and teenagers can easily raise barriers between couples; for example, disagreements on discipline methods, and on how much freedom and responsibility to give to the teen(s). Teenagers often become skilled at playing parents against one another, too, as some of you well know. It is also easy for parents to relive the adolescent period in their own lives through their teenage children. Problems and memories from that period in a parent's life are often projected onto the marriage relationship. If an adolescent rejects the values of parents, this can also affect the marriage. Couples begin to feel the psychological impact of aging and the crisis of the middle years. Jealousy of their maturing teenager is not uncommon, though usually unconscious. *If the marriage has been neglected* in favor of the children during the previous 15 or so years, *it is usually faltering by this time* and needs help!

There are several suggestions. First, couples should support each other at every opportunity. Give such important gifts as appreciation, respect, concern, and courtesy. Second, be aware of the pressures under which the other is functioning. For example, the husband may be worried about his job, and the wife may be worried about her life after the children leave home. Third, keep the communication lines open by finding times to talk and be alone. Talking reduces problems before they have a chance to build. Fourth, work to keep conflicts with teenagers from affecting the marriage itself. Fifth, begin planning more activities as a couple without the children. As teenagers associate more and more with their own friends, parents should offset this by developing their own activities together and with other couples. Sixth, give attention to personal appearance. The tendency of the middle years is to begin letting oneself go physically. This adversely affects a person's self-esteem, not to mention their health. Last, develop new hobbies, interests, and skills. Keep growing! This is particularly true for the wife who does not work outside the home. The leaving of the children will probably affect her more than the husband, whose work will probably be at its peak.[12]

Just remember Wesley's advice, parents! Your first responsibility in the home is *not* to the children but to each other. Fathers, the best thing you can do for your children is to love their mother well. Mothers, the best thing you can do for your children is to love their father well. When you do this, your marriage will become a ministry to your children, because *there is more than a casual connection between good marriages and successful child rearing!* Let's turn our attention now to the last and most important factor in Christian child rearing.

Informal Teaching Through Parental Example

I think one of the most gripping and challenging things John Wesley ever had to say about Christian parenting is found in a letter he once wrote to Miss Bishop dated July 17, 1781. It had to do with the power of a Christian example. He said, "As to you, I advise you, first, to be a Bible Christian yourself, inwardly and outwardly. . . . Then train up your children in the self-same way. Say to them, with all mildness and firmness, 'Be ye followers of me, even as I am of Christ.'"[13] Isn't that *powerful?* How many of us, parents, can say or would even want to say to our children, "Be ye followers of *me*"? And yet nothing is more important than for our sons and daughters to see Dad and Mom practice what they preach! In fact, we have no right whatsoever to ask our children to be or do something we're not willing to be or do ourselves. If so, we make a mockery of the Christian life, and no one will pick up on that faster than the boys and girls themselves.

Earlier in this chapter we read Deut. 6:7, which commands parents to teach their children the ways of God all through each day. What we didn't read was the verse before that. Deut. 6:6 says, "These commandments that I give you today are to be upon *your* hearts" (NIV, italics added). In other words, before parents ever concern themselves with their children's faith, they should concern themselves with their own faith. Of all the things we've talked about so far—ways to influence our children's Christian faith—there is *none* more important than the power of parental example!

There are three concepts about which we should think briefly, as they relate to this matter of parental example. They are the concepts of observational learning, "the hidden curriculum," and modeling.

Observational Learning

Observational learning is simply learning that takes place while watching or listening to others. The two types of observational learning are *imitation,* or behavior that is repeated, and *deferred imitation,* or behavior that is repeated at a later time. Research has shown that children pass through a series of stages in which they become more and more skilled at imitation. We are told that imitation of familiar actions begins as early as 4 months, whereas deferred imitation does not develop until about 18 months. This means that parents can expect their behaviors to be imitated by their children at a very early age.[14]

This matter of imitation was vividly illustrated to me one afternoon with my young son, Brandon. I was mowing the backyard, and right behind me was Brandon, pushing his little toy mower. After a while he noticed that I had a hand-kerchief hanging out of my back pocket to wipe the per-spiration. So what does he do? He runs into the house and comes out with this long, white towel stuffed into the back of his pants. He couldn't find a handkerchief, so the towel had to do. It was the funniest thing I've ever seen—this towel dragging the ground behind him like some long-tailed ani-mal. We continued our mowing until he noticed I was wear-ing a white headband, too. Into the house he runs once again, and this time emerges with one of his mother's dish towels. I tied it around his head, and off we went again—father and son looking exactly alike. Now that's imitation!

It shouldn't be difficult to understand the importance imitation has for our children's Christian faith. Children see our faith behaviors or the lack thereof, and they imitate our faith behaviors or the lack thereof. If they see and hear us pray, they will be more inclined to pray. If they do not see and hear us pray, they will be less inclined to pray. It's as simple as that! Obviously, learning by observation is important at all stages of faith development, but particularly so with stage one children (two or three years old to six or seven years old). Stage one faith has been defined as that "fantasy-filled *imitative* phase in which the child can be powerfully and perma-nently influenced by the *examples*, moods, actions and stories of [closely] related adults" (italics added).[15] The visible faith of parents is all-important!

The importance of observational learning to faith devel-opment can be further seen in the concept of "the hidden curriculum."

The Hidden Curriculum

Do you want to know something? We in the church are so accustomed to thinking of Christian education in terms of formal schooling and formal instruction that we forget all the informal, hidden factors that influence learning. Surprisingly, these informal, hidden factors—called "the hidden curriculum"—are often more influential than the formal factors.[16] For example, when parents teach one thing but live another, children are more likely to be influenced by what is *not* said—"the hidden curriculum"—than what is said. In other words, *religion is more caught than taught!*

Harry Emerson Fosdick, to whom I referred in chapter 1, tells how he hated mathematics in high school. He longed for the day he could pass his last exam and be done with it. Then in college he fell under the influence of one of the most inspiring personalities he had ever met. This professor just happened to be, of all things, a math professor! Fosdick ended up taking every elective this professor taught. The man could make even math contagious. Fosdick thought to himself that if a love for mathematics could be handed down by contagion, then so could other things—more important things—like religion! He concluded, "[Religion] is a fire that is passed from one life to another, not primarily by instruction, but by kindling."[17] I like that, don't you? And so family religion is like a fire that spreads from parents to their children.

If we were to cool down that metaphor and compare Christian education to an iceberg, the difference between "taught religion" and "caught religion" would probably look something like the following diagram.

This diagram does not mean formal teaching is unnecessary. After all, we just spent a whole chapter on that! It does mean that *what we are is more important than what we say!* This leads us to our third and final concept: modeling.

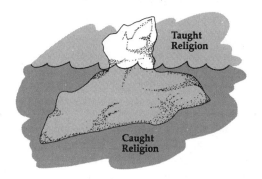

Modeling

Modeling means to set an example. The parent who models the Christian life is the parent who lives the Christian life and sets a good example. As a way of thinking about this, let's try another little exercise. Think back to your childhood and to those things you saw in your own parents while growing up. Write down five positive memories and five negative memories. For some of you, I realize the negative memories may be somewhat painful. I remember one young lady who did this, and the first thing she said was, "I didn't like what I saw." This may be how it is with you, but do the best you can. You might organize your paper like this:

Modeling

Five positive memories about my parents:

    1.

    2.

    3.

    4.

    5.

Five negative memories about my parents:

1.

2.

3.

4.

5.

Now, analyze each memory in relation to your *own* behavior as a parent. What are the differences? What are the similarities? Here's the reason for doing this. Our behavior has a profound effect on our children. That's nothing new to you, but this might be. It's easy to duplicate in our own family the same things we saw while growing up at home—even the negative things. There are many people who want their parenting style to be different from the way they were parented—in fact, more people want that than don't—but familiarity exerts a powerful pull![18] Once we see these same negative qualities in our own parenting and the effects they're probably having on our own children, then we can begin the process of eliminating them, with God's help.

More important than our knowledge of faith development, discipline, family worship, and life experiences, is our own Christian faith! If we are *really concerned* about bringing up our children in the Christian faith, then we will make our own Christian faith a priority. We will provide our children with a worthy role model. If not, then all the resources and materials in the world are not going to help us. This is because we parents are the only real material! We parents are the only real textbook! Everything else is secondary.[19] Nineteenth-century Christian educator Horace Bushnell (born 11 years after Wesley's death) put it like this:

> The . . . truth necessary to a new life, may possibly be communicated through and from the parent, being revealed in his looks, manners, and ways of life . . . for the

Christian scheme, the gospel, is really wrapped up in the life of every Christian parent, and beams out from him as a LIVING EPISTLE, before it escapes from the lips, or is taught in words.[20]

A *living epistle!* It would be hard to find a better definition of the Christian parent than that.

O God, I know I cannot communicate to my children something I do not possess myself. Forgive me for ever thinking or living differently. Help me to set my own Christian faith above all other priorities in my life. Help me to be Christian with my children. In Jesus' name and in His strength I pray. Amen.

At the beginning of the book, I asked you to perform an exercise called "The Family Blueprint: My Design for Disciple Making." The blueprint asked two big questions: "What do I want my child to become?" and "How can I seek to make that happen?" Perhaps you answered the first question easily enough but had trouble with the second. Hopefully this book has helped you answer that second question better. Why not do that exercise once again, and this time, really blueprint how you're going to go about bringing up your children in the Christian faith.

We close with this parting challenge from Mr. Wesley:

It is undoubtedly true, that if you are steadily determined to walk in this path; to endeavour by every possible means, that you and your house may thus serve the Lord . . . you will have need to use all the grace, all the courage, all the wisdom which God has given you; for you will find such hinderances in the way, as only the mighty power of God can enable you to break through. . . . But as you have begun, go on in the name of the Lord, and in the power of his might! . . . till every one of you "shall receive his own reward, according to his own labour!"[21]

Amen and amen!

DISCUSSION QUESTIONS

1. Discuss the idea that parents don't see themselves as Christian educators because they haven't been formally trained.

2. John Wesley believed that Christian parents should instruct their children both formally and informally. What are some examples of informal instruction?

3. What is the relationship of a good marriage to child rearing?

4. Discuss some of the ways couples can strengthen their marriage with children at:
   a. stage one
   b. stage two
   c. stage three

5. What is the *most important* factor in Christian parenting and why?

6. Write out and/or discuss the modeling exercise toward the end of the chapter.

Notes

PREFACE

1. James Dobson, *Family Under Fire: A Conference Book* (Kansas City: Beacon Hill Press of Kansas City, 1976), 59.

CHAPTER 1

1. Virginia Satir, *Peoplemaking* (Palo Alto, Calif.: Science and Behavior Books, 1972), 197.

2. Dorothy Corkille Briggs, *Your Child's Self-esteem: The Key to Life* (Garden City, N.Y.: Doubleday & Co., 1970), xiii-xiv; Thomas Gordon, *P.E.T.—Parent Effectiveness Training: The Tested New Way to Raise Responsible Children* (New York: New American Library, 1970), 1-2; Satir, *Peoplemaking,* 202-3.

3. Satir, *Peoplemaking,* 196-97.

4. Mary White, *Successful Family Devotions* (Colorado Springs: NavPress, 1981), 17.

5. Harry Emerson Fosdick, *The Power to See It Through: Sermons on Christianity Today* (New York: Harper & Brothers, 1935), 200.

6. Howard G. Hendricks, *Heaven Help the Home!* (Wheaton, Ill.: Victor Books, 1973), 21.

7. John H. Westerhoff III, *Bringing Up Children in the Christian Faith* (Minneapolis: Winston Press, 1980), 6-7.

8. William Barclay, *Educational Ideals in the Ancient World* (Grand Rapids: Baker Book House, 1959), 14-17.

9. Westerhoff, *Bringing Up Children,* 85-88.

10. *The Works of John Wesley,* 3d ed. (London: Wesleyan Methodist Book Room, 1872; reprint ed., Kansas City: Beacon Hill Press of Kansas City, 1978), 3:270.

11. *Webster's Ninth New Collegiate Dictionary,* s.v. "desideratum."

12. Wesley, *Works* 8:302; 3:270.

13. Ibid. 7:77.

14. John W. Prince, *Wesley on Education: A Study of John Wesley's Theories and Methods of the Education of Children in Religion* (New York: Methodist Book Concern, 1926), 134.

15. Wesley, *Works* 8:316.

16. Ibid.

17. Leslie F. Church, *The Early Methodist People* (New York: Philosophical Library, 1949), 231.

18. Percy Livingstone Parker, ed., *The Journal of John Wesley* (Chicago: Moody Press, n.d.), 297.

19. John A. Newton, *Susanna Wesley and the Puritan Tradition in Methodism* (London: Epworth Press, 1968), 120.

20. Rebecca Lamar Harmon, *Susanna: Mother of the Wesleys,* rev. ed. (Nashville: Abingdon Press, 1968), 64.

21. Church, *Early Methodist People,* 222.

22. Paul K. Jewett, *Man as Male and Female: A Study in Sexual Relationships from a Theological Point of View* (Grand Rapids: William B. Eerdmans Publishing Co., 1975), 37.

CHAPTER 2

1. Thomas A. Droege, *Faith Passages and Patterns,* ed. Allan Hart Jahsmann (Philadelphia: Fortress Press, 1983), 28, 44.

2. Leighton Ford, *Good News Is for Sharing* (Elgin, Ill.: David C. Cook Publishing Co., 1977), 148-49.

3. L. Howard Grimes, "The Bible and the Teaching of Children," *Perkins Journal* 31 (Fall 1977): 14.

4. John H. Westerhoff III, *Will Our Children Have Faith?* (New York: Seabury Press, 1976), 89-91.

5. Donald M. Joy, "Human Development and Christian Holiness," *Asbury Seminarian* 31 (April 1976): 25.

6. James W. Fowler, *Stages of Faith: The Psychology of Human Development and the Quest for Meaning* (San Francisco: Harper & Row, 1981), 123.

7. L. Joseph Stone and Joseph Church, *Childhood and Adolescence: A Psychology of the Growing Person* (New York: Random House, 1957), 108.

8. James W. Fowler and Sam Keen, *Life Maps: Conversations on the Journey of Faith,* ed. Jerome Berryman (Waco, Tex.: Word Books, 1978), 42.

9. Barbara Sweany McClinton and Blanche Garner Meier, *Beginnings: Psychology of Early Childhood* (St. Louis: C. V. Mosby Co., 1981), 193.

10. Mary M. Wilcox, *Developmental Journey: A Guide to the Development of Logical and Moral Reasoning and Social Perspective* (Nashville: Abingdon, 1979), 30-31.

11. Fowler and Keen, *Life Maps,* 42-44.

12. James Dobson, *The Strong-Willed Child: Birth Through Adolescence* (Wheaton, Ill.: Tyndale House, 1978), 171.

13. Fowler and Keen, *Life Maps,* 44-45.

14. Fowler, *Stages of Faith,* 135-37.

15. Westerhoff, *Bringing Up Children,* 40.

16. Fowler, *Stages of Faith,* 130-31; Fowler and Keen, *Life Maps,* 50-51.

17. Thomas H. Groome, *Christian Religious Education: Sharing Our Story and Vision* (San Francisco: Harper & Row, 1980), 237-38.

18. Fowler, *Stages of Faith,* 138.

19. Ibid., 151-73.

20. Joyce Huth Munro, "The Family: Cradle of Spiritual Development," *Review and Expositor* 75 (Winter 1978): 46.

21. Westerhoff, *Will Our Children Have Faith?* 89-99.

22. David Elton Trueblood, *Philosophy of Religion* (Grand Rapids: Baker Book House, 1957), 20.

CHAPTER 3

1. Church, *Early Methodist People,* 246.

2. Ibid.

3. Lawrence Stone, *The Family, Sex, and Marriage in England, 1500-1800* (New York: Harper & Row, 1977), 450-78.

4. Wesley, *Works* 1:386.

5. Ibid. 12:14.

6. Ibid. 1:385.

7. Prince, *Wesley on Education,* 108.

8. Wesley, *Works* 1:388-89.

9. Harmon, *Susanna,* 62, 115, 119.

10. Robert C. Monk, *John Wesley: His Puritan Heritage* (Nashville: Abingdon Press, 1966), 190.

11. Wesley, *Works* 1:392-93.

12. Ibid. 7:76.

13. Ibid., 79.

14. Ibid., 79-81.

15. Ibid., 86.

16. Ibid.

17. Ibid., 87.

18. Ibid., 92.

19. Ibid., 101.

20. Ibid., 102-3.

21. Ibid., 106.

22. Ibid. 13:476.

23. Ibid., 476-77.

24. Philip Greven, *The Protestant Temperament: Patterns of Childrearing, Religious Experience, and the Self in Early America* (New York: Alfred A. Knopf, 1977), 38, 49-50.

25. Wesley, *Works* 7:92-93.

26. Ibid., 93.

27. Ibid., 94.

28. Ibid., 95.

29. Ibid. 13:22.

30. Ibid. 7:81.

31. Ibid.

32. Prince, *Wesley on Education,* 86.

33. Wesley, *Works* 7:81-82.

34. Prince, *Wesley on Education,* 123-24.

35. Alfred H. Body, *John Wesley and Education* (London: Epworth Press, 1936), 50.

36. Wesley, *Works* 7:82.

37. Ibid., 82-83.

38. Prince, *Wesley on Education,* 125, 127-29.

39. Wesley, *Works* 12:449-50.

40. Richard Green, *The Works of John and Charles Wesley: A Bibliography,* 2d rev. ed. (London: Methodist Publishing House, 1906; reprint ed., New York: AMS Press, 1976), 45.

41. Ibid., 160.

42. Prince, *Wesley on Education,* 130-32.

43. Ibid., 133.

44. Wesley, *Works* 7:82.

CHAPTER 4

1. Haim G. Ginott, *Between Parent and Child* (New York: Avon Books, 1956), 114-15.

2. Ibid.

3. Dobson, *Strong-Willed Child,* 78.

4. Munro, "The Family," 48.

5. Stone and Church, *Childhood and Adolescence,* 254.

6. Dobson, *Strong-Willed Child,* 171.

7. James Michael Lee, "Discipline in a Moral and Religious Key," in *Developmental Discipline,* by Kevin Walsh and Milly Cowles (Birmingham, Ala.: Religious Education Press, 1982), 150.

8. W. Wayne Grant, *Growing Parents, Growing Children* (Nashville: Convention Press, 1977), 94-95.

9. Lee, "Discipline," 149-51, 217-18.

10. Grant, *Growing Parents,* 94-95.

11. Martin L. Hoffman, "The Role of the Father in Moral Internalization," in *The Role of the Father in Child Development,* 2d ed., ed. Michael E. Lamb (New York: John Wiley & Sons, 1981), 362.

12. Walsh and Cowles, *Developmental Discipline,* 45, 53-124.

13. Jane B. Brooks, *The Process of Parenting* (Palo Alto, Calif.: Mayfield Publishing Co., 1981), 42.

14. Gordon, *P.E.T.,* 49-94.

15. Fitzhugh Dodson, *How to Discipline with Love from Crib to College* (New York: New American Library, 1977), 61.

16. Gordon, *P.E.T.,* 105-20.

17. Brooks, *Process of Parenting,* 55.

18. Spencer Johnson, *The One Minute Father* (New York: William Morrow & Co., 1983), 19-42.

19. Dodson, *How to Discipline,* 9-10.

20. Johnson, *One Minute Father,* 47-59.

21. Dodson, *How to Discipline,* 41-43, 206.

22. Dobson, *Strong-Willed Child,* 46-47.

23. Rudolf Dreikurs and Vicki Soltz, *Children: The Challenge* (New York: Hawthorn Books, 1964), 77-78, 82.

24. Dodson, *How to Discipline,* 16-18.

25. Brooks, *Process of Parenting,* 79.

26. James Dobson, *Dare to Discipline* (Wheaton, Ill.: Tyndale House, and Glendale, Calif.: Regal Books, 1974), 56-58.

27. Dodson, *How to Discipline,* 21-22.

28. Brooks, *Process of Parenting,* 81.

29. Marian Marion, *Guidance of Young Children* (St. Louis: C. V. Mosby Co., 1981), 90, 92.

30. James Dobson, *Dr. Dobson Answers Your Questions* (Carmel, N.Y.: Guideposts, and Wheaton, Ill.: Tyndale House, 1982), 160-62.

31. Dobson, *Dare to Discipline,* 13.

32. Gordon, *P.E.T.,* 217, 237-42.

33. Dodson, *How to Discipline,* 82-84; Dreikurs and Soltz, *Children,* 301-5.

34. Gordon, *P.E.T.,* 152-53, 195.

35. Dreikurs and Soltz, *Children,* 145-54.

36. Wesley, *Works* 7:101.

37. Salvador Minuchin, *Families and Family Therapy* (Cambridge, Mass.: Harvard University Press, 1974), 68.

38. Howard J. Clinebell, Jr., and Charlotte H. Clinebell, *The Intimate Marriage* (New York: Harper & Row, 1970), 172.

39. Satir, *Peoplemaking,* 208-9.

40. Brooks, *Process of Parenting,* 86-89.

CHAPTER 5

1. White, *Successful Family Devotions,* 16-17.

2. Wesley, *Works* 7:81-82.

3. McClinton and Meier, *Beginnings,* 181-82.

4. Wesley, *Works* 7:82.

5. White, *Successful Family Devotions,* 93.

6. McClinton and Meier, *Beginnings,* 180.

7. Kieran Egan, *Educational Development* (New York: Oxford University Press, 1979), 36, 48-49.

8. Olive J. Alexander, *Developing Spiritually Sensitive Children* (Minneapolis: Bethany Fellowship, 1980), 35-37.

9. Wesley, *Works* 7:83.

10. Larry Christenson, *The Christian Family* (Minneapolis: Bethany Fellowship, 1970), 157-58.

11. James Dobson, *Straight Talk to Men and Their Wives* (Waco, Tex.: Word Books, 1980), 54-55.

12. Dorothy Jean Furnish, *Exploring the Bible with Children* (Nashville: Abingdon, 1975), 101-3.

13. Delores Curran, *Who Me? Teach My Child Religion?* (Minneapolis: Winston Press, 1981), 11. Author Curran recommends the *Arch Books* as some of the best Bible stories available for young children, and these can be used for dramatization of Bible stories.

14. Wilcox, *Developmental Journey,* 217.

15. Furnish, *Exploring the Bible,* 106-7.

16. Green, *Works,* 45.

17. Furnish, *Exploring the Bible,* 108-15.

18. David Elkind, "The Child's Conception of Prayer," in *The Child's Reality: Three Developmental Themes* (Hillsdale, N.J.: Lawrence Erlbaum Associates, Publishers, 1978), 27-45.

19. George Arthur Buttrick, *The Power of Prayer Today* (Waco, Tex.: Word Books, 1970), 51.

20. Alexander, *Developing Spiritually Sensitive Children,* 76.

21. White, *Successful Family Devotions,* 62-71.

22. Edward E. Thornton, "Raising God-Consciousness in the Family," *Review and Expositor* 75 (Winter 1978): 75.

23. Ibid., 84.

24. Charla Honea, *Family Rituals* (Nashville: Upper Room, 1981), 75.

25. Curran, *Who Me?* 8.

26. White, *Successful Family Devotions,* 88-115.

27. Curran, *Who Me?* 13.

28. Satir, *Peoplemaking,* 263-70.

29. Thornton, "Raising God-Consciousness," 85-86.

30. Evelyn Blitchington, *The Family Devotions Idea Book* (Minneapolis: Bethany House Publishers, 1982), 45-46.

31. White, *Successful Family Devotions,* 130.

CHAPTER 6

1. Curran, *Who Me?* 2-3.

2. Furnish, *Exploring the Bible,* 87-90.

3. Wesley, *Works* 7:82.

4. Ibid.

5. Curran, *Who Me?* 3-4.

6. Wesley, *Works* 7:78-79.

7. John M. Drescher, *If I Were Starting My Family Again* (Nashville: Abingdon, 1979), 9-14.

8. Paul Tournier, *The Strong and the Weak,* trans. Edwin Hudson (Philadelphia: Westminster Press, 1948), 45-46.

9. Satir, *Peoplemaking,* 227.

10. Clinebell and Clinebell, *Intimate Marriage,* 115-18.

11. Charles L. Allen, *Faith, Hope, and Love* (Old Tappan, N.J.: Fleming H. Revell Co., 1982), 157.

12. Clinebell and Clinebell, *Intimate Marriage,* 119-24, 161, 170.

13. Wesley, *Works* 13:38.

14. McClinton and Meier, *Beginnings,* 106-7, 118.

15. Fowler, *Stages of Faith,* 133.

16. Westerhoff, *Will Our Children Have Faith?* 6, 16-18.

17. Fosdick, *The Power to See,* 203-4.

18. Satir, *Peoplemaking,* 200-201.

19. Curran, *Who Me?* 129.

20. Horace Bushnell, *Christian Nurture* (New Haven, Conn.: Yale University Press, 1916), 14.

21. Wesley, *Works* 7:85-86.